THE BOOK OF JOB

A BIBLE STUDY GUIDE FOR MEN

THE BOOK OF JOB

A BIBLE STUDY GUIDE FOR MEN

VINCE MILLER

EQUIP PRESS

Colorado Springs

THE BOOK OF
JOB

Copyright © 2021 Vince Miller

All rights reserved. No part of this publication may be reproduced, distributed, or transmitted in any form or by any means, without prior written permission.

Published by Equip Press, Colorado Springs, CO

Scripture quotations marked (ESV) are taken from The ESV® Bible (The Holy Bible, English Standard Version®) copyright © 2001 by Crossway, a publishing ministry of Good News Publishers. ESV® Text Edition: 2011. The ESV® text has been reproduced in cooperation with and by permission of Good News Publishers.
Unauthorized reproduction of this publication is prohibited. Used by permission.
All rights reserved.

Scripture quotations marked (KJV) are taken from the King James Bible. Accessed on Bible Gateway at www.BibleGateway.com.

Scripture quotations marked (NASB) are taken from the New American Standard Bible® (NASB), copyright © 1960, 1962, 1963, 1968, 1971, 1972, 1973, 1975, 1977, 1995 by The Lockman Foundation, www.Lockman.org. Used by permission.

Scripture quotations marked (NIV) are taken from the Holy Bible, New International Version. Copyright © 1973, 1978, 1984, 2011 by Biblica, Inc.® Used by permission. All rights reserved worldwide.

Scripture quotations marked (NKJV) are taken from the New King James Version®.
Copyright © 1982 by Thomas Nelson, Inc. Used by permission. All rights reserved.

Scripture quotations marked (NLT) are taken from the Holy Bible, New Living Translation, copyright © 1996, 2004, 2015 by Tyndale House Foundation. Used by permission of Tyndale House Publishers, Inc., Carol Stream, Illinois 60188. All rights reserved.

Scripture quotations marked (NRSV) are taken from the New Revised Standard Version Bible, copyright © 1989 the Division of Christian Education of the National Council of the Churches of Christ in the United States of America. Used by permission. All rights reserved.

First Edition: 2021
The Book of Job / Vince Miller
Paperback ISBN: 978-1-951304-80-5
eBook ISBN: 978-1-951304-81-2

EQUIP PRESS
Colorado Springs

CONTENTS

HOW TO USE THIS HANDBOOK	7
HOW TO LEAD A GROUP	9
ABOUT VINCE MILLER	13
A SHORT INTRODUCTION	15
A GODLY RESPONSE TO EVIL AND SUFFERING	20
FOUR WAYS WE RESPOND TO SUFFERING	54
THREE QUESTIONS WE ASK WHEN WE GO THROUGH A CRISIS	83
HOW TO SPEAK UP WHEN IT'S OUR PLACE TO SPEAK UP	112
GOD INTERROGATES JOB: FOUR LESSONS	146

HOW TO USE THIS HANDBOOK

VIDEOS FOR THIS HANDBOOK

As you navigate this handbook, you will discover that the lessons are designed for use with online videos. These videos are viewable with a membership at our website: **www.beresolute.org**. You can use the videos for individual growth or with a group. Each lesson corresponds with the video of the same title. The best part is Vince Miller has structured the videos to provide relevant content for reflection and discussion so that you don't need hours to prepare. He does the work for you. Just push *play* on the video, and then reference this handbook.

THE METHOD

We believe in providing you with a full-scale game plan for growth. We are not just giving you content, but a *method* that has been field-tested with hundreds of thousands. While choosing the material is essential, we believe our step-by-step process is one of the best for producing a spiritual change. We have tested the components in each session and how they link together within a series or group of series that complement ongoing growth. Our goal is to produce life change. In each lesson, you will notice clear goals and outcomes, purposeful reflection and discussion questions, a rich study of God's Word, and practical application with actionable steps to be taken. While we know you need content, we hope our commitment to this method deepens their relationship with Christ and with one another.

THERE IS MORE IN THIS SERIES

Remember, once you finish this series there are many others that follow it and build upon it. Don't do just one series, do them all!

HOW TO LEAD A GROUP

ONE | GATHER YOUR TEAM

Assembling a team is critical. A team should include a pair of leaders who become the *"On-Site Hosts"* for the experience. We believe working in pairs is by far the most practical approach. Remember, every pilot needs a wingman.

TWO | RECRUIT PARTICIPANTS

Don't stress: whether you recruit half a dozen or a hundred, the content will be useful. We have found the best recruiting success comes from finding people who are hungry to grow spiritually. While the content is suitable for any believer of any age, the best recruit is the one who wants to be there, someone who hungers for the Word of God, and occasionally some food as well!

THREE | MAKE SURE EACH PARTICIPANT HAS A HANDBOOK

Our guides may be purchased in the online store: www.beresolute.org. These are your guides for taking notes, guiding a dialogue in your group, and recording outcomes at the end of every lesson. Handbooks also include other materials for additional development. You will want one for each lesson series.

FOUR | ONLINE RESOURCES FOR LEADERS

If you have purchased online video access with your membership, you can view all the material. You will be able to listen to audio recaps, watch the videos, read the full transcripts, and even review past lessons. There are also training articles and videos online to help you lead your group.

FIVE | MORE MATERIAL & VINCE MILLER

At Resolute, we are not just providing content. We are inviting you to an experience. Here are other tools you can utilize.

- Need a devotional? Read the Daily Devotional: www.beresolute.org/mdd
- Need prayer? Vince Miller will personally pray for you: www.beresolute.org
- Need a speaker? Invite Vince Miller to speak: beresolute.org/vince-miller
- Need help as a leader? Contact Vince Miller directly at vince@beresolute.org

It is our goal to partner with you and your ministry. We want to resource you with tools that compliment your development as a follower and a leader.

SIX | CONNECT SOCIALLY

We would love to have you join our social networks. Head to our home page and connect with us on Twitter, LinkedIn, and Facebook.

ABOUT VINCE MILLER

Vince Miller was born in Vallejo, California, and grew up on the West Coast. At twenty, he made a profession of faith while in college and felt a strong, sudden call to work in full-time ministry. After college and graduate school, he invested two decades working with notable ministries like Young Life, InterVarsity Christian Fellowship, the local church, and in senior interim roles. He currently lives in St. Paul, Minnesota, with his wife Christina and their three teenage children.

In March 2014, he founded Resolute out of his passion for discipleship and leadership development of men. This passion was born out of his personal need for growth. Vince turned everywhere to find a man who would mentor, disciple, and develop him throughout his spiritual life. He often received two answers from well-meaning Christian leaders: *either they did not know what to do in a mentoring relationship, or they simply did not have the time to do it*. Vince learned that he was not alone. Many Christian men were seeking this type of mentorship relationship. Therefore, he felt compelled to build an organization that would focus on two things: ensuring that men who want to be discipled have the opportunity and that they have real tools to disciple other men.

Vince is an authentic and transparent leader who loves to communicate with men and has a deep passion for God's Word. He has authored several books, and he is the primary content creator of all Resolute content and training materials.

A PERSONAL NOTE FROM VINCE

I pray this experience will benefit your life and your spiritual journey. I hope you will do three things as you engage. First, that you will be receptive to the Word of God. I love that we dig into the Bible each time we meet. At Resolute, the Bible is not an afterthought. It is the means of discovering God and transformation. Second, lean into the community of this experience. Build friendships, share transparently, and have conversations that go beyond the superficial. Third, apply what you have learned. Take an action item with you every week, knowing that one small step weekly leads to success over a lifetime.

Keep moving forward,

A SHORT INTRODUCTION

Job is a book dedicated to the exciting topic of suffering.

It's the story of a blameless and upright man who appears to be undeserving of the suffering he endured. You see, most people don't have a problem with suffering when it happens to the disobedient and the unrighteous. In fact, we love it when someone who has done injustice receives justice, especially when they have been unjust to us. We love it when a person who cuts us off in traffic gets pulled over a few miles up the road. It gives us this strange sense of satisfaction. Yet when a righteous man suffers for doing right we sometimes struggle with this reality. We have a problem with it because we see it as unjust and unfair. Therefore, it causes us to ask some big questions about the justice of God.

This is the topic of the book of Job.

Before we dive in, let's do a brief summary of this 42-chapter book.

Job, (pronounced *Jobe*) who is the central character of this book, is a man of profound character. He appears to be the prototype of a godly man, husband, father, and leader. In fact, he has gained a great name for himself on earth and in heaven.

But the plot thickens.

In the beginning of the book we get a peek behind the divine curtain at a conversation held in the heavenlies. It's a conversation to which Job is not privy. We hear a dialogue between God and a fallen angel. His name — Satan. Satan begs God to give him a chance to test the character and faithfulness of Job. In chapters 1-3 we watch and listen as the limits of Job's faith are tested.

Then in chapters 3-42, which is the rest of the book, we read about one day in the life of Job. Yes, one single day, and on this day, we listen to three major conversations.

The first conversation is with three friends who come to console Job and offer their advice. Their names are Eliphaz, Bildad, and Zophar. Their conversation with Job consumes the majority of the book (chapters 4-31). They console him one at a time with a series of looping conversations. They each take a turn and then Job responds to each, and it loops almost three times in its entirety. First Eliphaz speaks and then Job responds. Then Bildad speaks and then Job responds. Then Zophar speaks and then Job responds. This cycle repeats a second and a third time, except each time the advice from the friends gets shorter and Job's responses get longer. Basically, the sum of their advice is this, *"You have sinned. God is punishing you. You need to repent."* They blame his suffering on some known or unknown personal sin and call for his repentance so the suffering will stop. I think they do what anyone would do from a natural perspective: they come to the wrong conclusion thus give the wrong advice, primarily because they are not privy to the divine conversation. And while all this plays out, we wonder if Job is going to break.

The second conversation is an exchange between Job and Elihu (found in chapters 32-37). Elihu is a younger man who has been listening to the conversation among the four men. When he speaks, we discover that he's pretty angry with the counsel the three men give to Job. But in addition, he's also with angry with Job. He feels Job's response is self-righteousness, that Job, in defense of himself, has made too much of his righteousness. The essence of Elihu's speech is powerful. It starts like an angry rant and then transitions into praise of the greatness of God. The sum of his speech is this: *"God is sovereign. Man cannot comprehend him. And our righteousness does not dictate his action."*

The third and final conversation is one between God and Job. This is definitely the apex of the book. It's found in chapters 38-42. Essentially God picks up where Elihu left off. There is a whirlwind and then God speaks. And God's initial statement sums it all up. God says this in Job 38:2-3:

> "Who is this that darkens counsel by words
> without knowledge?
> Dress for action like a man; I will question you,
> and you make it known to me."
>
> **JOB 38:2-3**

Finally, at the end of the book, Job comes to his senses about his self-righteousness. He realizes God is God, and he is not, and therefore he confesses and repents. And of course, in the end a blessing abounds in Job's life. It a greater blessing than even he had before, but it comes with a greater understanding of first, God's righteousness and second, of his own unrighteousness.

So, there's a quick summary.

I think the book of Job is one amazing book. It addresses some of the greatest questions of all time. Questions you might be wrestling with right now. It provides incredible clarity for men looking for the answers to these questions. We are going to try and tackle this book in five lessons:

- Lesson One: A Godly Response to Evil and Suffering
- Lesson Two: Four Ways We Respond To Suffering
- Lesson Three: Three Questions We Ask When We Go Through A Crisis
- Lesson Four: How To Speak Up When It's Our Place To Speak Up

A SHORT INTRODUCTION

- Lesson Five: Four Lessons From God's Interrogation Of Job

I want to challenge you to read through this book of the bible in its entirety. I will be condensing this study to only five lessons, which addresses some of the main content of the book. While I know you will love our content, I also want you to love the Bible and the God of the Bible who gave us this book. I have also included in this study guide some opening and closing discussion questions for group discussion or personal reflection that will help you dig into the topics a little more. And following each lesson, I have included some daily devotionals that will give you something to reflect on daily. So grab a Bible, a journal, your handbook, and let's dig into lesson one of the Book of Job.

A GODLY RESPONSE TO EVIL AND SUFFERING

OPENING QUESTIONS:
- What's a question you would like to ask God about evil and suffering? Why this question?
- How have you had to endure evil or suffering in your life?
- What are some responses people have to evil and suffering? Why such a variety?

LESSON ONE

In this session we are going to look at most of the first chapter of Job. We are going to attempt to answer one of the hardest questions that mankind asks of God, which is this:

Why do bad things happen to good people?

And we are going to do this by looking at Job chapter one and take note as four scenes unfold in Job's life.

SCENE ONE | A SELFLESS SPIRITUAL LEADER

The first few verses of Job 1 set the scene.

> There was a man in the land of Uz whose name was Job, and that man was blameless and upright, one who feared God and turned away from evil. There were born to him seven sons and three daughters. He possessed 7,000 sheep, 3,000 camels, 500 yoke of oxen, and 500 female donkeys, and very many servants, so that this man was the greatest of all the people of the east. His sons used to go and hold a feast in the house of each one on his day, and they would send and invite their three sisters to eat and drink with them. And when the days of the feast had run their course, Job would send and consecrate them, and he would rise early in the morning and offer burnt offerings according to the number of them all. For Job said, "It may be that my children have sinned, and cursed God in their hearts." Thus Job did continually.
>
> **JOB 1:1-5**

So, the first few words of this book tell us several things about Job. First, where he lived. Second, the nature of his character. Third, the extent of his wealth. Fourth, the size of his family.

I think what's most interesting is how this section concludes. It focuses on the selfless concern Job had for his family's spiritual well-being. It is very illuminating to hear about Job's heart for his family. We see that he is more concerned about his family's rightness with God than the accumulation of his wealth. This contrast displays the true motive of Job's heart.

Tis is spiritual leadership. Which is a great lesson for men, husbands, fathers, and leaders. I want to note two marks of his spiritual leadership that are exposed in this section of text.

MARK ONE | SPIRITUAL LEADERS HAVE UNSEEN SPIRITUAL PRIORITIES

The text reads, "*he would rise early in the morning.*" So we see that his first morning thought is about his family's relationship with God. In this situation, and on this day, his children are on his mind. He is genuinely concerned for them. And remember: Job was a busy man. In verse three the author states he was one of the wealthiest and largest ranchers in all the East. Yet even though the busyness of his business was calling, he set this busyness aside. He had something else to address before he got to his business; it was the *unseen* spiritual leadership of his family.

We should have the same kind of priority for the spiritual leadership of our family. It should be our first waking thought. Yet I know this is not true for so many husbands and fathers. This is because we have other pressing priorities at the beginning of our day. We feel compelled to pursue our careers and provide financially for our family to the exclusion of spiritual provision. Thus, our spiritual focus and spiritual leadership becomes an afterthought, if any thought at all. This needs to change for us as spiritual leaders in the home. Beyond feeding our egos and our pocket books in the pursuit of our career, we must first feed our family spiritually. We can do this very simply by praying for them at the start of each day, just like Job does in this instance. Yes, it is unseen. Yes, it requires discipline. Yes, it means putting off some other apparently more pressing issues. But this is at the core of Job's leadership. It's not a leadership tactic. It's simply Job starting his day humbly by calling on the God that leads him to help him lead his family. Job understands that God is the ultimate leader, and he is not. Therefore he calls on God's leadership. We should be doing the same, which means starting our day with a priority for God and his leadership, even when no one sees it. This is what great spiritual leaders do.

MARK TWO | SPIRITUAL LEADERS RECEIVE FORGIVENESS AND SHARE IT WITH OTHERS

Listen to verse five and imagine the moment if you will.

"Job would send and consecrate them, and he would rise early in the morning and offer burnt offerings according to the number of them all."

JOB 1:5

In ancient times, burnt offerings were required as a means of atonement for sin. What someone would do is bring a flawless animal from their herd or flock and offer their life on the altar for their sin. This type of atonement for sin served to remind a follower of their depravity. And you will notice here that Job did not offer a sacrifice for himself, which would have been the normal practice. But instead, he acts very selflessly and offers a series of ten burnt offerings one for each of his children out of concern for them and the possibility that they might have sinned.

Knowing this should be very convicting for men leading a household. Christianity should be flooded with men like this. Men who think about themselves less and have a great spiritual concern for others, especially those within our families.

This type of selfless spiritual leadership only occurs when a man is touched by the boundless riches of God's forgiveness and wants others to experience this same forgiveness. Some men need to begin with learning to receive God's forgiveness. We might have to stop rejecting the forgiveness of God. You see God forgives you. But you must choose to accept this forgiveness. I know so many men who wrongly believe God will never forgive them, which hinders their spiritual growth and leadership. But receiving God's forgiveness of us is what fuels a selfless desire for the forgiveness of others. It fuels our selfless spiritual leadership. Selfless spiritual leadership is not about focusing your leadership on others. No: selfless spiritual leadership is about focusing on God, receiving his grace, mercy, love, and forgiveness and then letting the overflow of what we have received to spill out on others. This is a hard lesson to learn but in this text we see that Job knows this. How? He has received his forgiveness but each day he wants the same for his children.

Thus we have two great marks of spiritual leaders. **Spiritual Leaders Have Unseen Spiritual Priorities** and they **Receive Forgiveness and Share It With Others.**

SCENE TWO | A DIVINE PROPOSITION

Now I am not going to say a lot on this point because we are going to come back to this scene in the next session, but I want you to listen to one specific verse here. Verse eight reads this way:

> *And the Lord said to Satan, "Have you considered my servant Job, that there is none like him on the earth, a blameless and upright man, who fears God and turns away from evil?"*
>
> **JOB 1:8**

This is a significant moment, because we get to see something we don't usually get to see. It's a look behind the divine curtain. Even Job is not privy to this conversation. It's a divine meeting about him. And in this moment God appears to invite Satan to test his finest man. And thus, we are set up for what happens next.

SCENE THREE | A FIRST DISASTER

I call this the *first* disaster because there are two. And this first one has a number of parts. Here is the story in verse 13-19:

> *Now there was a day when his sons and daughters were eating and drinking wine in their oldest brother's house, and there came a messenger to Job and said, "The oxen were plowing and the donkeys feeding beside them, and the Sabeans fell upon them and took them and struck down the servants with the edge of the sword, and I alone have escaped to tell you." While he was yet speaking, there came another and said, "The fire of God fell from heaven and burned up the sheep and the servants and consumed them, and I alone have escaped to tell you." While he was yet speaking, there came another and said, "The Chaldeans formed three groups and made a raid on the camels and took them and struck down the servants with the edge of the sword, and I alone have escaped to tell you." While he was yet speaking, there came another and said, "Your sons and daughters were eating and drinking wine in their oldest brother's house, and behold, a great wind came across the wilderness and struck the four corners of the house, and it fell upon the young people, and they are dead, and I alone have escaped to tell you."*
>
> **JOB 1:13-19**

So, four messengers bear four devastating messages. It's a combination of both natural disaster and physical harm that test Job's faith in God. He is tested when he experiences the theft of his possessions, the killing of his workers, a fire that burns animals and servants, and a wind that took his children as well. This is a moment that we would not wish on anyone righteous or unrighteous.

What is challenging about this disaster is that God permits it. We clarified this in point two. And so, this raises the question:

"Why do bad things happen to good people?"

This is a very challenging question, if not the most challenging question anyone will ever ask. It is challenging because we must wrestle with the collision between two things. First, the existence of evil. Second, the existence of a sovereign God. As humans who reason within the limits of human understanding, we have a hard time reconciling the two. Therefore, we look for ways to make sense of them. And we make sense of this question by doing one of two things. Either **reducing the existence of evil** or **reducing the existence of a sovereign God**. So let's talk about both.

First | A Reduction of Evil

Do you even realize that the very question itself attempts to reduce evil?

Again, the question is this: *"Why do bad things happen to good people?"* The question itself supposes that we, or someone, is *"good."* It assumes we are not evil, and therefore we do not deserve to suffer.

But the Bible never states we are *"good."* In fact, the Bible says quite the opposite. That we are *bad* in the worst way. Roman 3:23 says this:

"For all have sinned and fall short of the glory of God."

This verse declares that evil and sin are no small issue. Evil is a massive problem in all forms. It's a problem with both **natural evil**, in the form of natural disaster, and **moral evil**, in the form of sin and selfishness that lives within a man. Yet we want to assume we are *"good,"* because we don't want to be on the hook for sin and evil. We would prefer to assume we are *"good,"* or *"mostly good,"* with little culpability for sin and the suffering that comes from it.

But if we assume we are *"good,"* or *"mostly good,"* then we have to wrestle with what we read in James 2:10-11.

> *For whoever keeps the whole law but fails in one point has become guilty of all of it. For he who said, "Do not commit adultery," also said, "Do not murder." If you do not commit adultery but do murder, you have become a transgressor of the law.*
>
> **JAMES 2:10-11**

The point is this. We may think we are good, but really, we are not. We are only good according to our measure of goodness, not according to God's measure of goodness. Therefore, we have a flaw in our question that attempts to reduce the evil in us. And we will come back to this.

Second | A Reduction of God

So another way we try to make sense of the problem of evil is by reducing God.

Coming back to the original question, let's recognize that this question is being asked of God. We could ask it this way.

"Why do you (God) one who claims to be all-powerful and all-loving, let bad things happen to good people?"

This question is very theological. But we have to remember it's a deeply *personal* question. We ask this most often when we go through a time of great suffering. Even I have asked it. We usually ask it because we feel our suffering from a natural or moral evil is underserved and maybe unbearable. So we want to know why God is doing it.

For example, we ask this when a disease sweeps across the world and takes millions of innocent lives. Or when an evil person murders an innocent person or child. In these moments, we turn to God and ask: *Why?*

What we are trying do is make sense of why people suffer and why God allows it. Yet so many Christians in seeking the answer will reduce God's sovereignty. In these tragic moments, we try to find ways to *"save God"* of his sovereignty because we don't want him to be responsible for suffering. We do not want God to be *"on the hook"* for evil or any kind of suffering in this life. So we reduce him.

But ultimately a sovereign God is responsible for everything. This includes the allowance of evil and suffering. Now this is not to imply that God does evil, but allows evil, both natural and moral evil. Yet he retains his sovereignty over all evil. And we do not need to help God, save God, or reduce God in order to make sense of evil. In fact, Job does not reduce God's sovereignty in his own suffering. Just look at four transactions in chapter one that elevate God's sovereignty.

First, Job 1:8:

> *"And the Lord said to Satan, "__**Have you considered my servant Job**__, that there is none like him on the earth, a blameless and upright man, who fears God and turns away from evil?""*
>
> **JOB 1:8 (EMPHASIS ADDED).**

This is God and Satan in a verbal interchange. Do not be confused about this. God called a meeting and Satan showed up because he was required to be there. Remember, Satan is a fallen angel who is allowed by God to walk and roam the earth.

What you see in this is God's sovereign power, authority, and control. As they confer, God presents Job as a viable option, not because he hates Job, but because he sees that Job is blameless and upright and he want to use Job to put Satan in his place. Is God out of control here? No. God is acting and speaking in his sovereignty. He is not previously sovereign and now not as he gives permission to Satan to tempt a man.

Second, Job 1:11 reads:

> "**But stretch out your hand** [states Satan] and touch all that he has, and he will curse you to your face."
>
> **JOB 1:11 (EMPHASIS ADDED)**

Here Satan is testing God. Satan is trying to get God to do something that he knows God can do. Because, get this, Satan knows that God is totally sovereign. In God's total sovereignty, Satan knows that God can stretch out his hand and destroy all he has. Of course, this does happen. But Satan does it because God allows it. Is God still sovereign in this moment? The answer is yes!

Third, Job 1:16 reads:

> "While he was yet speaking, there came another [servant] and said, "**The fire of God** fell from heaven and burned up the sheep and the servants and consumed them, and I alone have escaped to tell you.""
>
> **JOB 1:16 (EMPHASIS ADDED)**

Even the servants communicating this awful news recognize that God sent the fire. They call it *"the fire of God."* Now we can try to explain this away by calling this a natural disaster, or volcanic explosion of some kind, but remember natural evil and moral evil are not outside the sovereign control of an all-powerful God.

Fourth, Job 1:21:

> "And [Job] said, "Naked I came from my mother's womb, and naked shall I return. **The Lord gave, and the Lord has taken away**; blessed be the name of the Lord."
>
> **JOB 1:21 (EMPHASIS ADDED)**

Note this: Job has no problem with the fact that God allowed this. He knows that God is in sovereign control. So, if Job does not have a problem with this, neither should we. In fact, that he perceives it this way results in something beautiful. It results in praise. And we sing about this all the time in a well-known song, **"Blessed Be The Name."**

We should note that as the story progresses, Job's view of his righteousness gets a little too high and his view of God gets a little too low. But here, in this moment, his view of God is very high. And because his view of God is very high, God is proved right, and Satan is proved wrong—again. This means that when we try to reduce God's sovereignty by letting him off the hook for moral and natural suffering and evil, we may miss the opportunity to shame Satan and shout to God.

So, let's agree that evil exists and God exists. And that we do not want to reduce the problem of evil or reduce the sovereignty of God. If we can keep from doing these two things, then we can come up with a simple answer to our question:

Bad things happen to all people because our world reaps the effects of our disobedience to God in garden.

Romans 5:12 says this:

"Therefore, just as sin came into the world through one man, and death through sin, and so death spread to all men because all sinned."

The bad news is that one act of disobedience by Adam resulted in suffering for all mankind. This means that we suffer for Adam's sin. But just when you think you are an innocent sufferer because Adam sinned and you didn't, you have to face off with Roman 3:23.

"For all have sinned and fall short of the glory of God."

This means that even though we might think we are an innocent sufferer, we are not. We are just as guilty as Adam. We are not exempt from sin. Nor are we exempt from suffering due to sin—even when suffering from someone else's sin. Everyone has sinned. Everyone suffers. In fact, the only person who is able to legitimately ask the question, *"Why do bad things happen to good people?"* would be Jesus Christ. He was the only truly good or righteous man to live. He was sinless in every way. And yet he too suffered at the hand of sinful and unrighteous men. Was this fair? Well, in one respect "yes." Because he was subject to a natural law and living in a world of sin and suffering. I think in another respect "no," in that he was righteous and did not deserve to suffer, but he chose to do so. He suffered evil as the only good and righteous man for the purpose of bringing glory to a sovereign God.

I think this helps us to arrive at an answer to our original question. It could be correctly asked this way. *"Why do bad things happen to a good person. The only good person. Jesus Christ?"*

Here is the answer to the right question. Bad things happened to a Jesus Christ the only righteous man to magnify God's glory.

SCENE FOUR | A GODLY RESPONSE

This scene is amazing. God is magnified through Job. And it's beautiful. Here is the text. I have already read a portion of it. Job 1:20-22:

> *Then Job arose and tore his robe and shaved his head and fell on the ground and worshiped. And he said, "Naked I came from my mother's womb, and naked shall I return. The Lord gave, and the Lord has taken away; blessed be the name of the Lord." In all this Job did not sin or charge God with wrong.*
>
> **JOB 1:20-22**

Job does not have a problem with God being sovereign. Nor does he have a problem with Satan perpetuating evil and suffering. In fact, at this moment, his view of God is very high. God's sovereignty is more than the sum of his possessions, property, workers, land, money, wealth, and even the children who he prayed for. I know this is hard to fathom. It's almost hard to believe. But remember, Satan suggested that Job believes in God only because God has protected him. Satan thinks that Job is going to cave once all these things are gone. That all these things were the focus of his worship. But that is not the case. Job's response proves Satan wrong. We discover that Job has faith only in God and not his possessions, property, workers, land, money, wealth, or even his children.

So, we have with a lot to think about. I want you to consider this: What one thing is preventing or impeding your faith in God?

- *Could it be a question?*
- *Could it be a suffering?*
- *Could it be a possession, person, or problem in this life?*

Take some time to seriously reflect on this and consider what you might need to lay aside to live a life of greater faith. Faith in a great and sovereign God. One that would bring you to the point that you could make this proclamation.

The Lord gave, and the Lord has taken away; blessed be the name of the Lord.

The great preacher and teacher R.C. Sproul once said this:

"Ultimately the only answer God gave to Job was a revelation of Himself. It was as if God said to him, "Job, I am your answer." Job was not asked to trust a plan but a person, a personal God who is sovereign, wise, and good. It was as if God said to Job: "Learn who I am. When you know me, you know enough to handle anything."

REFLECTION & DISCUSSION QUESTIONS:

- Can you proclaim or sing the words that Job proclaimed in your suffering: "Blessed be the name of the Lord?"
- We will either **reduce evil** or **reduce God** to make sense of suffering. Which do you tend to do?
- What issues do you need to address in your suffering right now?
- Is there something you need to do to respond differently than you have in the past?

DEVOTIONALS FOR JOB 1

A RIGHTEOUS MAN

> *There was a man in the land of Uz whose name was Job, and that man was blameless and upright, one who feared God and turned away from evil.*
>
> **JOB 1:1**

Job's story has such a strong start and a strong end. It's the middle of the story (spanning 42 chapters) that is rather shocking to read. But in these first verses, we get a picture of the type of man that Job was. The author declares that he was blameless and upright one who feared God. In other words, he was a man of unusual moral and spiritual character. He clearly stood out among men in his time.

Was he a perfectly moral and spiritual man? No. But Job did possess an unusual moral and spiritual character that resulted in natural blessing. It was so widely recognized that even otherworldly characters, like Satan, were witness to it.

In the coming devotionals, we will look deep into Job's challenges, friendships, and the divine interactions that surround a period of suffering in his life. But for now, I want you to consider this question: Are you a follower who strives for moral and spiritual righteousness?

I know you haven't been morally or spiritually perfect in the past. I know you will never be perfect by your own strength. But in the grace and perfection of Christ, are you striving after moral and spiritual righteousness? Are you really striving? If not, consider this: what one thing do you need to stop, start, or continue to strive another day after the righteousness which Jesus strove hard for you?

ASK THIS: Are you striving after moral and spiritual righteousness?

DO THIS: What one thing do you need to stop, start, or continue to strive another day after the righteousness which Jesus strove hard for you?

PRAY THIS: God, I confess that I am not perfect by my own strength. But I want to strive harder because you strove hard for me. God accept my confession and offering today. Give me the desire to strive hard in your grace.

2 MARKS OF A GREAT FATHER

> *And when the days of the feast had run their course, Job would send and consecrate them, and he would rise early in the morning and offer burnt offerings according to the number of them all. For Job said, "It may be that my children have sinned, and cursed God in their hearts." Thus Job did continually.*
>
> **JOB 1:5**

As a young man, I grew up without a father in my home. Therefore, when I eventually became a father, I wondered if I would make a very good one myself. This text provides some great wisdom. It clarifies two marks of great fathers.

First, great fathers make spiritual leadership a priority. Let me reiterate what I have said before, Job woke early in the morning. His first thought is about his family. And let's keep in mind, Job was busy. In verse three, the author states he was one of the wealthiest and largest ranchers in all the East. Yet even though his business and the busyness was calling, it waited. His priority on this morning was the spiritual leadership of his family. On this day, it was his children that came to mind. This is a definitive mark of a great father. He cares first about the spiritual leadership of his family.

Second, great fathers are marked by their selfless offerings. Notice that Job did not offer a sacrifice for himself, which would be expected in this situation. Rather, out of concern for his children, he offers a sacrifice for them. This is rather unusual but highly commendable. It gives us insight into how much he cared about his children and their ongoing relationship with God.

And so, in this one verse, Job raises the bar for all Christian fathers. Here are two questions to consider:

- *What adjustments do you need to make in your schedule for your family?*
- *What spiritual sacrifices do you need to make for the care of your family?*

Adjust today. Whether you are a father or not. Set a new pattern and example for coming generations.

ASK THIS: What adjustment or sacrifice do you need to make today?

DO THIS: Make a small adjustment and share your commitment below.

PRAY THIS: God, I want my family and children to know you, not how busy I am or how much I work. Help me prioritize and reprioritize my life and align it to things that matter for eternity.

SATAN'S PRESENT RULE

> *The Lord said to Satan, "From where have you come?" Satan answered the Lord and said, "From going to and fro on the earth, and from walking up and down on it."*
>
> **JOB 1:7**

Here we encounter a meeting of cosmic proportions. God and Satan meet and have a divine conversation. And the subject matter is one man in particular — Job. It's clear from this divine meet-up that God rules the infinite limits of the universe, and in comparison, Satan walks the confines of the earth.

While this meeting is disturbing for some, let make sure we understand the authority of Satan in this life.

- *Satan is a fallen angel who rebelled against God. (Luke 10:18, Isaiah 14:12-15)*
- *Satan is given the freedom to rule the present world. (Ephesians 6:12)*
- *Satan does not have authority over God-fearing believers. (1 John 3:8, James 4:7)*
- *Satan does have authority over those who believe in him. (Ephesians 2:2)*
- *Satan uses lying and deception to persuade belief in him, which gives him his power. (Genesis 3:1, John 8:44, 2 Corinthians 11:14)*

- *Satan will be in ongoing conflict with Christians until the time is complete. (Ephesians 6:11-16)*
- *Satan will be destroyed at the end of this time. (Revelation 20:10)*

So this behind-the-scenes look into this divine meeting should not concern us who are believers in God. It is only a reminder of these facts:

- *That we live in a fallen world corrupted by humanity's disobedience to God.*
- *That our disobedience to God gives authority to Satan.*
- *That we need a God to save us from our sin, selfishness, and Satan's control.*
- *That belief in God results in new and eternal life.*
- *That until Satan is destroyed, we must battle with his lies and deception.*

So today, if you are a follower of Jesus Christ, don't be concerned about this cosmic conversation. Just get out there today and engage in the battle. Watch carefully for those lies and deceptions the enemy will throw at you and guard against them with God's truth.

ASK THIS: What common deceptions do we passively or actively embrace in our time?

DO THIS: Pray that God will reveal deception in others and you.

PRAY THIS: God, please convict me when I see deception in this life. Please also convict me when I embrace deception myself. Cleanse me of all unrighteousness.

THE SELECTED MAN

> *And the Lord said to Satan, "Have you considered my servant Job, that there is none like him on the earth, a blameless and upright man, who fears God and turns away from evil?" Then Satan answered the Lord and said, "Does Job fear God for no reason? Have you not put a hedge around him and his house and all that he has, on every side? You have blessed the work of his hands, and his possessions have increased in the land. But stretch out your hand and touch all that he has, and he will curse you to your face."*
>
> **JOB 1:8-11**

This proposition is almost inconceivable to our human minds. What loving Father would willingly direct Satan to inflict suffering on a faithful son? How could God lower the "hedge" of protection around one of his most faithful children? Yet, this subtly suggests that God is responsible for the pain and suffering of this life when he's not. We are responsible. It's our sin and selfishness that ushered suffering into this world. Therefore many a righteous man will suffer at the hand of godless disobedience.

What's unique here is that we get this momentary glimpse of what is transpiring behind the scenes: a look at a conversation between God and Satan.

Yet couldn't this also be interpreted as glorious? Yes, glorious! Glorious in that God saw something in Job that would endure longer than other common men. A man of uncommon faith. Uncommon willingness. Uncommon endurance. Therefore God selected him for affliction that many could not bear. And in the end, he would become one of the greatest stories of suffering of all time. It is the story of one morally upright man suffering injustice at the hand of Satan. It's the story of a man stripped of everything: children, possessions, property, and power and enduring horrific physical pain. It's one man selected by God to become one of the greatest stories ever told, second only to Jesus Christ, God's Son, who suffered sinlessly. Could there be anything more glorious than suffering at the hand of unrighteousness and enduring for the sake of righteousness?

Rather than be disturbed by this conversation, maybe it's more appropriate to hear the wonderful pride in God's voice as he says to Satan:

"Have you considered my fearless and faithful son Job? He will suffer through anything for me, and he will never give up because he knows your deceptive ways, and he fears only me."

It should be an honor to suffer for the sake of Christ. So here is a question for you today. Do you choose to suffer for the Gospel and name of Jesus Christ today?

ASK THIS: What suffering are you facing today?

DO THIS: Suffer better today than you have in the past.

PRAY THIS: God, while I don't want to be selected for suffering, but if I am, help me to suffer better.

4 MESSAGES OF TRAGEDY

> *Now there was a day when his sons and daughters were eating and drinking wine in their oldest brother's house, and there came a messenger to Job and said, "The oxen were plowing and the donkeys feeding beside them, and the Sabeans fell upon them and took them and struck down the servants with the edge of the sword, and I alone have escaped to tell you." While he was yet speaking, there came another and said, "The fire of God fell from heaven and burned up the sheep and the servants and consumed them, and I alone have escaped to tell you." While he was yet speaking, there came another and said, "The Chaldeans formed three groups and made a raid on the camels and took them and struck down the servants with the edge of the sword, and I alone have escaped to tell you." While he was yet speaking, there came another and said, "Your sons and daughters were eating and drinking wine in their oldest brother's house, and behold, a great wind came across the wilderness and struck the four corners of the house, and it fell upon the young people, and they are dead, and I alone have escaped to tell you."*
>
> **JOB 1:13-19**

I cannot imagine what this day was like. Four messengers with four compounding tragic messages. While I have had some bad days, I can confidently assert that I have never experienced anything like this (to this point) in my life.

Yet some families have been touched by these types of experiences. They have experienced murder at the hands of wicked and corrupt people. Or they have experienced natural disasters that have taken family members from them. And these moments are unsettling. They are unsettling for those directly impacted but also for those who are mere observers.

When this happens, we all ask one big question: "Where is God during all this?" This is a common question. I have asked it. We ask this question because a human loss by what appears to be unjust means incites reflection on more than just this life. It drives us to consider the question of God.

What's interesting in this instance is that we know exactly *"where God is during all this."* He, our Sovereign God, is in heaven. God permitted this situation. He gave Satan the freedom to test this man, not a sinful man but a righteous man. Earlier in the chapter he is described as blameless and upright. While we weigh this thought and consider our big question let's not forget that this world is Satan's domain. That it's Satan who struck this man with these catastrophes by the hand of men who did his evil bidding. It's our sin that invited this type of suffering into this world in the first place. So while God maintains sovereign authority, Satan works overtime to find people who will worship him during this age. He will use any means necessary to persuade disbelief in God.

So as we continue Job's story, we will discover that he was a man who maintained faith through challenging moments. When enticed he never sided with Satan. This raises a better and far more important question for people of God: will your faith stand strong in those moments you encounter great tragedy?

ASK THIS: Is your faith standing strong?

DO THIS: Ask God for faith and strength to endure one more day.

PRAY THIS: God, give me a supply of greater strength and faith today.

I WILL PRAISE

> *Then Job arose and tore his robe and shaved his head and fell on the ground and worshiped. And he said, "Naked I came from my mother's womb, and naked shall I return. The Lord gave, and the Lord has taken away; blessed be the name of the Lord."*
>
> **JOB 1:20-21**

By the end of this first chapter Job is stricken with events that no man wants to encounter. His possessions, cattle, servants, and ten children are taken from him. While we don't know exactly what this moment felt like to Job, you've probably experienced devastation on a far less significant level. But notice how Job responds. He stood up, stripped naked, shaved his hair, fell to the ground stripped of everything, and worshipped God. While this was completely natural for a man who was in mourning, his next response is inspiring and awesome.

"The Lord gave, and the Lord has taken away; blessed be the name of the Lord."

What brings a man to assert this? Here are the two factors. Factor one, Job is certain that God is sovereign and Satan is not. Factor two, his circumstances never determined his faith. His possessions, land, cattle, servants, family, and finances were not the object nor the means of his faith — God was. So when these mere things were taken from him, his faith remained intact, unaffected by circumstances.

So here are two questions we need to ask ourselves in light of all that is happening in the world and our lives:

- *Do you believe that God is still sovereign?*
- *Do you have faith in God or circumstance?*

Take a moment to reflect on these questions and then consider what you might need to confess for you to be able to make this proclamation:

"The Lord gave, and the Lord has taken away; blessed be the name of the Lord."

ASK THIS: Do you believe that God is still sovereign? Do you have faith in God or circumstance?

DO THIS: Confess to God what is hindering your faith in him.

PRAY THIS: God, my faith has been altered by the challenging circumstances of this life. I bring these circumstances to you, knowing that you are still sovereign and that they are in your care. Increase my faith today. Reveal yourself in the circumstances of my day.

EXONERATED

In all this Job did not sin or charge God with wrong.

JOB 1:22

This is theologically stunning. Primarily because when man encounters tragedy we go straight to questioning God. But remember it is not humanity who is on trial here. Humanity is fallen. The earth is Satan's fallen domain. Rather, Satan has put God on trial. Satan suggested that Job's faithfulness was dependent on God's blessing and dependent on the protection God had afforded him. But God knows better. The protection and blessing are removed and Satan is proved wrong—again. While most men in this situation would have gone immediately to questioning God and charging him with wrongdoing Job does not. Job never sins or charges God with any wrong.

After reading this it makes me wonder if right now in our life there is a divine discussion occurring behind the scenes? If supernatural powers convene to discuss our faithfulness? I wonder, as our protections and blessings fall if God is looking down on us with a smile as he proclaims:

"Stay in the battle brothers! Satan is furious, but the victory is mine. Let's prove this guy wrong!"

ASK THIS: What battle are you fighting today?

DO THIS: Prepare your heart and take up arms against the enemy, and battle!

PRAY THIS: God, give me strength to war with the enemy and his schemes. I am weak and need your strength today!

FOUR WAYS WE RESPOND TO SUFFERING

OPENING QUESTIONS:

- How do you most typically respond to suffering?
- How do people in your family of origin respond to suffering?
- Would you be willing to change if you found out your response to suffering needed some adjustment?

LESSON 2

In this life suffering creates a plethora of questions for all of us. In fact, in my work with men over many years, I have come to learn that suffering is a major stimulus for change in a man's life. Unfortunately, we learn more from pain and suffering than we ever will from success. We learn from suffering that we are acutely selfish. We have this preference for doing life our way. But when our way does not work out, we experience pain and suffering. This is because the Bible teaches that pain and suffering result from disobedience to God.

Well known author and speaker Lee Strobel once said this:

Moral evil is the immorality and pain and suffering and tragedy that come because we choose to be selfish, arrogant, uncaring, hateful and abusive.

While suffering feels *"bad"* it does teach us some pretty remarkable things about ourselves and God. For me, suffering is where I have learned most of life's greatest lessons. Suffering in school, career, marriage, parenting, and through personal sin I have discovered things about God and others that I could have never learned without suffering. This is because when I suffer, I look for any means possible to discontinue the pain, address the issues, and seek healing in hopes of not repeating the process ever again. The great preacher Charles Spurgeon once said this:

I am certain that I never did grow in grace one-half so much anywhere as I have upon the bed of pain.

Let's look at how to respond to suffering. We must recognize we each respond differently to it. This depends greatly on a number of factors. For example, how prepared we are for suffering, the connection we have to it, past experiences with it, and even the intensity and length of the suffering itself.

Given this we return to Job. In chapter two we are going to encounter four responses to suffering. One response from Satan;

one response of Job's wife; one response from Job; and one response from Job's three friends.

FIRST | THE RESPONSE OF SATAN

Job 2:4-8 reads this way:

> Then Satan answered the Lord and said, "Skin for skin! All that a man has he will give for his life. But stretch out your hand and touch his bone and his flesh, and he will curse you to your face." And the Lord said to Satan, "Behold, he is in your hand; only spare his life." So Satan went out from the presence of the Lord and struck Job with loathsome sores from the sole of his foot to the crown of his head. And he took a piece of broken pottery with which to scrape himself while he sat in the ashes.
>
> **JOB 2:4-8**

I am so grateful that in scripture we get this behind-the-scenes glimpse of just how devious, malicious, and relentless Satan can be. I believe this gives us a greater understanding of what is behind Job's suffering. And it helps us to have a greater understanding of what might be going on behind our suffering. Satan works overtime to incite a selfish response from Job. Even though he lost round one he is not going to quit. And this is Satan's *modus operandi*, his M.O. This time he turns away from his previous strategy of taking possessions and people, to a personal attack, one that inflicts his body with unbelievable physical suffering.

Job is stricken with boils from head to toe. His hair follicles are infested with bacteria causing irritation and swelling that result in pus forming underneath the surface of his skin. The stretching of his skin becomes so painful it makes his bones writhe in pain. Seeking relief, he breaks open the boils with fragments of pottery, which results in only temporary relief. The open wounds now emit an awful stench and now these open lesions get infected, dirty, and become infested with worms. As his skin heals it hardens and then breaks open every time he moves. His clothes stick to him, and during sleep he is tormented with night terrors. We really don't know how long Job suffered through this situation, it could have been weeks or as many as nine months, but we do know this: his situation was horrendous.

Please hear this: Satan will always respond to suffering with more suffering. This is his M.O. and it's not going to change. He will not quit. He will keep coming. He will always tempt us by doing the same three things he does here. Here are three aims of Satan's temptations.

Three Aims of Satan's Temptations

First, his **temptations are aimed at turning us against God**. Satan states very openly that his purpose here is to get Job to *"curse God to his face."* And listen carefully! Every temptation is a move against God. Satan's setting us up to turn toward a selfish desire which is a move that is in direct opposition against God. He wants us to turn from biblical truth to our truth which is to tell God to buzz-off and butt-out of our life.

Second, Satan's **temptations are aimed at pushing our limits**. Satan said to God, *"But stretch out your hand and touch his bone and his flesh."* What we hear is that Satan is not going to stop after one failed attempt. He going to try again and again and again. Sometimes he's going to be relentless.

Third, Satan's **temptations are aimed at attacking our weaknesses**. Everyone experiences temptation, but we are not all tempted exactly the same way. This is because Satan is going to attack you where you are weakest. He is coming after your compulsions, your vices, your irritations, and the things you admire, revere, or idolize. If you struggle with a form of pride, he's coming after that. If you struggle with a form of materialism, greed, or selfishness you bet he's coming after that. This is because he knows what is common to you.

As you encounter suffering, you need to remember that Satan is right there, too, and he's ready to tempt you to turn against God, push you to your limits, and by attacking you in your unique way.

SECOND | THE RESPONSE OF A SPOUSE

Job 2:9 reads:

> *Then his wife said to him, "Do you still hold fast your integrity? Curse God and die."*
>
> **JOB 2:9**

Now before we get too judgmental here of what Job's wife declares we need to note a few things about her. First, that this is the only place she is mentioned in the book of Job. Second, it's the only time she speaks in the book of Job. Third (and I think most importantly), we need to remember she is suffering, too. Job's not the only person has lost everything. She has as well. And now she watches as her husband is being tormented with bodily sores from head to toe.

There are two things interesting about what she says in this single verse.

First, that she makes almost the same assertion that God makes about Job. Listen to what God says to Satan in Job 2:3.

"Have you considered my servant Job, that there is none like him on the earth, a blameless and upright man, who fears God and turns away from evil? **He still holds fast his integrity***..."*

Both God and Job's wife notice the same quality in Job. He will not compromise. He is an uncompromising man. Which is very commendable. It's a quality to be desired.

Second, the next part of what she says is almost the same as what Satan is suggesting Job will do. Satan's proposition to God is that if God touches his skin and his flesh, now he will compromise his integrity. And Satan asserts that, *"he will curse you to your face."*

I find it very interesting that his wife's only comments mirror components of the discussion that happened between God and Satan. Partly what God says, and partly what Satan says.

I have found this principle at play in my life. That sometimes God-fearing people can offer wonderful advice. And that sometimes God-fearing people can offer tragic advice. And in suffering, we need to remind ourselves to not let our guard down with those who we think can be trusted. Because sometimes these genuine God-fearing people can offer advice that is genuinely wrong. As J.I. Packer once said:

"A half-truth masquerading as a whole truth becomes a complete untruth."

THIRD | THE RESPONSE OF THE PERSECUTED

Job 2:10 reads,

> But [Job] said to [his wife], "You speak as one of the foolish women would speak. Shall we receive good from God, and shall we not receive evil?" In all this Job did not sin with his lips.
>
> **JOB 2:10**

Notice the strength of Job's clarity to be lucid enough through all his pain and suffering to still respond to his wife. This is profound. He is not trying to be condescending but rather confident of her character and virtue. He essentially says to her, *"You are not like other women so don't speak like one of them."* Next, notice how Job is still trusting in the sovereignty of God. At no point does he seem to question God's power and sovereignty in his suffering. Most men would cave, but not Job. He accepts his suffering from God as if it came from God. Finally, notice Job does not *"sin with his lips."* This is not suggesting that Job has no sin, but only that Job did not sin to deserve this suffering nor that he sinned with his mouth as he suffered at that moment.

Clearly Job is a man of exceptional integrity and perseverance. His response to his wife and to God demonstrates remarkable understanding, trust, and faith in God. He accepts his suffering as his call and is willing accept it as his present calling. Charles Stanley once said this:

"When you become consumed by God's call on your life, everything will take on new meaning and significance. You will begin to see every facet of your life – including your pain – as a means through which God can work to bring others to Himself."

And I believe this is why Job responds in the way he does here.

FOURTH | THE RESPONSE OF FRIENDS

Job 2:11-13 reads:

> *Now when Job's three friends heard of all this evil that had come upon him, they came each from his own place, Eliphaz the Temanite, Bildad the Shuhite, and Zophar the Naamathite. They made an appointment together to come to show him sympathy and comfort him. And when they saw him from a distance, they did not recognize him. And they raised their voices and wept, and they tore their robes and sprinkled dust on their heads toward heaven. And they sat with him on the ground seven days and seven nights, and no one spoke a word to him, for they saw that his suffering was very great.*
>
> **JOB 2:11-13**

This is the premier example of what to do when you have a friend who is suffering through personal loss and personal challenges. These men got three things right:

First, **they went to him**. I have learned over the years that presence is a real ministry. Sometimes we underestimate presence. The ministry of presence is done by visiting a friend in the hospital, attending a funeral, and stopping by to offer condolences. It communicates something that a card, phone call, or email will never communicate. Never take this granted. It is not quickly forgotten.

Second, **they wept with him**. Some of us lack friends these types of friends. But we need friends who empathize with us. And we need to empathize with others. Empathy is powerful. We can be far to calloused in this life. Even detached from people. But these men got this this right. They felt his pain, and traveled long and far just to weep with him.

Third, **they sat quietly with him**. These three men gathered around him for seven days before they spoke a word. They commiserated with their brother in silence. I think this is beautiful. It demonstrates commitment to Job as a man, husband, father and leader.

They got these three things right. They went to him, wept with him, and sat with him. But, as we soon will discover, when they opened their mouths they became a serious problem.

So today whether you are going through suffering or know someone who is, I hope you take away something actionable from this incredible chapter and these responses. Maybe you needed to be reminded of Satan's relentlessness. Maybe you needed be reminded to cautiously accept advice from those close to you. Maybe you needed to be reminded by Job to hold fast to God's sovereignty and trust in God. Or maybe you needed to be reminded to be a great friend to someone who needs a friend.

Regardless, know this: *everyone* suffers. Everyone gets a turn. So be ready to respond, and I pray your response will be godly.

JOB

REFLECTION & DISCUSSION QUESTIONS:

- Where you at all surprised by Satan's response that led to Job's suffering?
- Which of the three aims of Satan's temptations captured your attention?
- Did it surprise you that Job's wife's response was mixed with God's truth and Satan's lie?
- So Job's three friends were not all that bad in the beginning. They did three things right. They went to him, wept with him, and sat with him. Which do you need or want in your suffering?

DEVOTIONALS FOR JOB 2

DIVINE COUNSEL

> *Again there was a day when the sons of God came to present themselves before the Lord, and Satan also came among them to present himself before the Lord.*
>
> **JOB 2:1**

Because we live in a natural world, these divine meetings appear unusual to us. Yet they shouldn't be. A supernatural God created us. In fact, as followers, we declare belief in a divine supernatural and spiritual being, and the unseen spiritual world is just as real as this physical experience. Because God is the God of order, he convenes a meeting. (One that might run a little more effectively and efficiently than the ones we attend, even with a fallen angel in attendance—Satan.)

Two important reminders here. First, we are reminded that God is orderly. He gathered the "sons of God" (or "angelic beings") together for some check-in or presentation meeting. In this, we assume that God commands the order of all things in the spiritual world, and he does this in an orderly fashion. Second, we are reminded that God is in control. Notice that even Satan is not "off the hook" for attending this routine angelic gathering. This assumes that God continues to command authority over fallen creation and Satan, who has been given dominion over the earth.

So as you walk into the chaos of your day, be reminded that there is a divine spiritual world. And while this world looks to be out-of-control, know this: God is one of order, and nothing in this life is out-of-his-control. Even Satan and his workers of lawlessness.

ASK THIS: What appears out-of-control in our world?

DO THIS: Remember, God is in control. It might do you well to say this a few times to yourself throughout this day or even write this down on a note on your desk — GOD IS IN CONTROL!

PRAY THIS: God, I shout from the depth of my heart — "You are in control!" when I feel I am not.

HE JUST WON'T STOP

> *And the Lord said to Satan, "Have you considered my servant Job, that there is none like him on the earth, a blameless and upright man, who fears God and turns away from evil? He still holds fast his integrity, although you incited me against him to destroy him without reason."*
>
> **JOB 2:3**

Have you had one of those days, weeks, or months where you did not know if the trials and tests were ever going to end? Of course you have. That might be today. And as you are trying to make sense out of your suffering, know that God may see it as unreasonable as well. Did you see how God responded to Satan here? He declared. "You incited me against him to destroy him without reason." See that? Without reason!

But as you are spending all this time reasoning about your suffering, you might need to reason about something else as well. There is a great God who still rules all things. A God with absolute sovereign control. A God who is not tempted or threatened by Satan's relentless requests as he roams the earth. A God who knows just how much you can handle. A God who may see in you the courage, temperance, perseverance, and endurance of Job. A man who "there is none like him on the earth, a blameless and upright man, who fears God and turns away from evil?"

So today, as you consider the trials and temptations that won't stop, do two things for me. First, stop reasoning about out why Satan is tempting you without reason. He's pretty unreasonable. Second, start reasoning about why God has chosen you. Search long and hard for why God may have chosen you. Like Job, he may have chosen you because he sees something noble in you that will become a witness for others through this season of suffering. And then once you think you have identified this quality, pray for its increase in you. And then stand strong.

So remember, when you have those days where Satan just will not stop, you are chosen by God, not by Satan! That God may have chosen you for an extraordinary story. One of great victory over evil and sin that will be used in this life to display God's glory, a story that God is writing right now in you.

ASK THIS: What positive characteristic does God see in you that uniquely qualifies you for your present suffering?

DO THIS: Focus less on what Satan is doing in your suffering and more about what God is doing through you.

PRAY THIS: God, what you see in me, declare out loud to me. Give me more of what I need to endure this season. May your glory be displayed through my suffering and weakness. Turn this season into a story of your greatness and a testimony for others.

WHEN IT GETS PERSONAL AND PAINFUL

> *Then Satan answered the Lord and said, "Skin for skin! All that a man has he will give for his life. But stretch out your hand and touch his bone and his flesh, and he will curse you to your face."*
>
> **JOB 2:4-5**

So Satan lost round one big time. It was a bit of an embarrassment for him. But we discover here that Satan doesn't give up easily. He's not a quitter. In fact, he will not stop tormenting creation until the day God banishes him to Hell. Till then, he is free to walk and roam the earth. And because Satan acts in his nature, which is in rebellion with God, he will do anything to create chaos in God's created order. He will use physical suffering to persuade humanity to act in rebellion with God.

Round two gets a lot more personal. Satan asks for permission to attack Job's flesh and inflict physical pain. It's not just emotional pain like we saw in round one. Round two is about causing a skin infection that ignites the nerve endings of his body.

I believe Satan chooses this means of suffering because he knows we have a preference for comfort. And he knows that comfort is often the reason we are driven to God. We come to God to seek the comforts of salvation from pain caused by sin. And as we come, God saves us. He saves us from our sin and eternal suffering. But salvation from temporal pain is not guaranteed in this life. It's not guaranteed until that last day. So Satan uses temporal pain to sway disbelief in God and the comforts of his salvation. He essentially uses discomfort to get us to question a comforting God. And for some, this results in disbelief.

So today, if you are encountering physical and personal pain, don't let a desire for temporal comfort drive you from spiritual comfort in God. Temporal pain of any kind, like a torn tendon, a broken bone, aching joints, skin disease, or even cancer it is only a reminder that one day God will give us new bodies. The apostle Paul said this:

> *Behold! I tell you a mystery. We shall not all sleep, but we shall all be changed, in a moment, in the twinkling of an eye, at the last trumpet. For the trumpet will sound, and the dead will be raised imperishable, and we shall be changed. For this perishable body must put on the imperishable, and this mortal body must put on immortality.*
>
> **1 CORINTHIANS 15:51-53**

ASK THIS: What temporal pain are you suffering, and how is it causing you to question the comfort of God?

FOUR WAYS WE RESPOND TO SUFFERING

DO THIS: Standfast in belief about the spiritual comforts promised by God and the eventual resurrection of a new body.

PRAY THIS: God, be glorified in me.

PUSHED TO THE LIMITS

*And the Lord said to Satan,
"Behold, he is in your hand; only spare his life."*

JOB 2:6

At first, we may read this divine invitation as a little disturbing. You're probably considering the same question that I instantly ask, which is, "Why is God allowing Satan to torment Job?" Because as we read ahead, we discover that Job is about to be stricken boils from the top of his head to the bottom of his feet. It's an honest question.

But here's a small caveat. Consider this. If we both trust the one pushing us to our limits and understand the purpose behind the pain, are we compelled to ask the same question the same way? Are we? For example, when a trusted coach pushes us to train harder so that we can perform better against an opponent, are we compelled to ask the question, "Why are they tormenting me?" Maybe. But if we train hard under that coach and he leads us to a victory, we make two discoveries. First, we discover a new level of trust and connection with our coach. Second, we discover that our coach had a plan and purpose in the pain. And afterward, all the "torment" is worth it.

So in Job's situation, if we knew this trial would draw him closer to God and be would be used to cleanse him from self-righteousness while simultaneously using a mortal man to defeat Satan and becoming one of the great stories of suffering and victory of all time, would you then ask the same question the same way? Maybe, but at least now you have a lot of perspective.

Maybe the better question is this: *"Am I willing to suffer to know God and his purposes in my life, so that others might benefit from my story well into the future?"*

Take a few moments to consider this question today. If you happen to be right in the middle of a trial, try to identify what God is teaching you about him or his purposes.

ASK THIS: What has God taught you, or is God currently teaching you through your trial(s)?

DO THIS: Ask the right question. *"Am I willing to suffer so that I might know God and his purposes in my life?"*

PRAY THIS: God, I am challenged by my trial today. It is consuming my mental, emotional, and physical energy. Please reveal your purpose and plan to me. Please give me a view of the end. Please give me the endurance and strength to hang on. I pray you will be victorious over the enemy in my life, and may your name be glorified in me!

UNBELIEVABLE SUFFERING

> *So Satan went out from the presence of the Lord and struck Job with loathsome sores from the sole of his foot to the crown of his head. And he took a piece of broken pottery with which to scrape himself while he sat in the ashes.*
>
> **JOB 2:7-8**

Job has become entirely covered by boils. Boils are these painful, pus-filled blisters under the skin caused by infected hair follicles. Follicles get infected with bacteria, fill with pus, stretch the skin, rupture, and then scar over. A cluster of boils is called a "carbuncle." And Job was covered by one big carbuncle.

I think it is important not to diminish the pain and discomfort that Job endured. In fact, Job chronicles some details of this experience in the chapters that follow. Listen to how he describes it:

- *My flesh is clothed with worms and dirt; my skin hardens, then breaks out afresh. (Job 7:5)*
- *Then you scare me with dreams and terrify me with visions. (Job 7:14)*
- *My breath is strange to my wife, and I am a stench to the children of my own mother. (Job 19:17)*

- *My bones stick to my skin and to my flesh. (Job 19:20)*
- *The night racks my bones, and the pain that gnaws me takes no rest. (Job 30:17)*
- *With great force my garment is disfigured; it binds me about like the collar of my tunic. (Job 30:18)*
- *My skin turns black and falls from me, and my bones burn with heat. (Job 30:30)*

This wasn't normal suffering. This was extraordinary suffering! But given all this Job says this later in his chronicle.

---

*For I know that my Redeemer lives,
and at the last he will stand upon the earth.
And after my skin has been thus destroyed,
yet in my flesh I shall see God,
whom I shall see for myself,
and my eyes shall behold, and not another.*

JOB 19:25-27

I don't know if you have experienced this in your life yet. But sometimes, unbelievable suffering results in some of the most unbelievable praise. What are you praising God for today? And as you praise, consider what God has brought you through that has resulted in this praise.

ASK THIS: What are you praising God for today?

DO THIS: Know your Redeemer lives.

PRAY THIS: God, challenges surround me. Please show me and others that you are greater than all of them. Redeem me, my Redeemer!

WHEN IT'S TIME TO CORRECT YOUR SPOUSE

> *Then his wife said to him, "Do you still hold fast your integrity? Curse God and die." But he said to her, "You speak as one of the foolish women would speak. Shall we receive good from God, and shall we not receive evil?" In all this Job did not sin with his lips.*
>
> **JOB 2:9-10**

Before we get too far into these verses, let's remember the three things about Job's wife we covered in the previous chapter. First, this is the only place in the 42 chapters of the book that Job's wife is mentioned. This means we only get one small glimpse of her life. Second, it's the only time she speaks. This means we only get this one myopic view of all the things she may have said to her husband and that she might have said many wonderful and supportive things as well. Third, let's keep in mind that Job is not the only person who has lost everything. She has too. She is going through financial and personal devastation and lost ten children she gave birth to and raised into adults. And now, she watches as her husband lives in physical torment covered in boils.

With these reminders let's turn to the question: When is it time to correct your spouse?

It's time to correct when a spouse persuades us to compromise spiritual integrity. Let's recognize that there are times in a marriage that one spouse will enter a negotiation with the other spouse. What they are trying to do is strike a "deal" that both benefits them and the other person. For example: if you do "this" then I will do "that," which will benefit us both. These negotiations lead to deals that result in compromises. It could be a compromise of any kind: financial, travel, parenting, recreational, or otherwise. Sometimes we agree to these deals to expedite a process, appease a spouse, or get what we want. But sometimes, these compromises jeopardize our spiritual integrity. And usually, they are a little less obvious. But this one by Job's wife is obvious. She says, "Curse God and die!" So, honey, we don't want to do that.

So how do we know we have made a spiritual compromise? The answer simple. We have made a spiritual compromise when we have exchanged a high view of God for a high view of ourselves. Note what Job said to his wife. "Shall we receive good from God, and shall we not receive evil?" He's proclaiming a very high and sovereign view of God over all things, good and evil. He's right to do this. He's willing to fight for it. He's pointing out the obvious result of her statement, that spiritual integrity is only worth it when times are good, not when times are bad. Job responds quite insightfully with this very high view of God. He could have said this. "If God is only God of the good, then what good is God?"

So today, you may encounter a moment you have to correct somebody, even a spouse. The key is this: if you must compromise, don't compromise your high view of God. Let God be God, of good and the bad.

ASK THIS: Have you struck any deals that have compromised your spiritual integrity?

DO THIS: If so, correct course!

PRAY THIS: God, forgive me for not having a high view of you. Help me to stand up and speak out on behalf of what is right and righteous.

THE MOST COMFORTING THING TO SAY

> *Now when Job's three friends heard of all this evil that had come upon him, they came each from his own place, Eliphaz the Temanite, Bildad the Shuhite, and Zophar the Naamathite. They made an appointment together to come to show him sympathy and comfort him. And when they saw him from a distance, they did not recognize him. And they raised their voices and wept, and they tore their robes and sprinkled dust on their heads toward heaven. And they sat with him on the ground seven days and seven nights, and no one spoke a word to him, for they saw that his suffering was very great.*
>
> **JOB 2:11-13**

So now, in the story of Job, we get to meet his three friends. You'll notice that from a distance, they witness the despair of his situation. Job physically looks almost unrecognizable to them. There is a short customary greeting, and then finally, they just sit with him — speechless — in the ministry of presence.

Over 30 years ago, I recall encountering a similar moment. My grandfather, who was my mentor, contracted terminal cancer. He was pretty successful at hiding it from many of us, until he was admitted into the hospital, where he spent the final few days of his life. At the time, I was away at college, and it had been several months since I had last seen him. I quickly headed home, went directly to the hospital, and found him lying alone in a hospital bed. Like Job, he was almost unrecognizable. His skin was yellowed. His eyes were sunken back into his head. The hair was gone from his body. His muscle had deteriorated and appeared to be hanging from his bone. As I walked in, we talked for a few minutes until he was more than exhausted. After which, I pulled up a chair and just sat with him. For the next five hours, that's all I did. And for five hours, I watched him die while listening to the ambient noise of his gasping for air. Gradually the space between the gasps increased until finally, he took his last breath.

You know, sometimes the most comforting thing we can say to people who are suffering is nothing at all. In fact, I commend these three friends for sitting in silence with him for seven days. The ministry of presence is powerful. Sometimes it's more powerful than anything that can be said. Besides, people say some pretty stupid things to people who are grieving or going through significant suffering. In fact, after this seventh day, these three friends are going to open their mouths. And as soon as they do, they are going to give some awful advice because they have come to some wrong conclusions about God, what God was doing, and why. However, these men, right at this moment, do exactly the right thing. They K.M.S. (Keep Mouth Shut). And it's commendable.

So don't undervalue the ministry of presence by speaking into a suffering person's life. Instead, sit with them! It's powerful!

ASK THIS: Who do you need to sit with today?

DO THIS: K.M.S. and value presence over proclamation.

PRAY THIS: God, thank you for walking planet earth and coming close to us when we felt far off. May I do the same for others.

THREE QUESTIONS WE ASK WHEN WE GO THROUGH A CRISIS

OPENING QUESTIONS:

- What has been the most challenging crisis you have faced in your life?
- What questions did you ask when you went through this crisis?
- Were any of your questions aimed at God?
- Did you find any answers on the other side of the crisis?

LESSON 3

When we begin our relationship with Christ, we sometimes assume that rest of our lives are going to be struggle free. And yes, God does rescue us from the eternal punishment due from our sin. But this does not mean that life is going to be free from struggle. In fact, Jesus told us to anticipate the struggle. To anticipate that following him would include unbelievable challenges. That following him requires us to daily deny ourselves, take up our cross, and follow him. He never promised an easy life, but one that would present all kinds of problems. Career problems, family problems, and health problems. And sometimes these problems all happen at one time.

For some these problems will result in a crisis of faith. And this crisis is filled with some big questions about God. This is one thing I appreciate about the story of Job. It helps us to see and resolve a number of the big questions we all ask.

Questions like:

- *Where is God?*
- *Is he still in control?*
- *Why is this happening to me?*
- *Does God still care?*
- *Does he see my situation?*
- *Does he hear my prayers?*
- *Did I do something wrong to deserve this?*
- *Is there something I need to do to address the issue?*
- *When will this suffering end?*

I want to take a look at a few of these questions. To seek the answers to them we will turn to the dialogue between Job and his three friends found in Job chapters 4-31. Since a lot of this discussion is repetitive in nature, and many of the questions are repeated in a variety of ways, I want to look at only a few of the questions presented. Three in all. I believe they are the three questions we will ask when we go through a crisis.

QUESTION ONE | IN MY CRISIS, DO I STILL BELIEVE GOD IS SOVEREIGN?

In Job 9:19, Job says:

> *If it is a contest of strength, behold, he is mighty!*
> *If it is a matter of justice, who can summon him.*
>
> **JOB 9:19**

In Job 12:13, Job says:

> *With God are wisdom and might;*
> *he has counsel and understanding.*
>
> **JOB 12:13**

When we begin our journey with God, we tend to have a high trust in God's sovereignty. This means we believe that God is fully in control. Mostly because we need him to be in control. We embrace the truth that he has to be the ruler and we cannot. This is because we have tried our hand at leading our life and realized that we were incapable. Therefore, we surrendered our life to him, meaning we have given him control.

But then something happens. We encounter a challenge in our life. This challenge, whatever it might be (like a career, marriage, or financial challenge) elicits a response from us, usually an emotional response. These emotions result in feelings of doubt, concern, anxiety, and frustration that cause us to question God's working. Sometimes our initial faith in God begins to waver because we have some newfound concerns, situational concerns that we didn't have before. Regardless, they are always questions about one thing: questions about God's sovereignty in our life. Suddenly the strength of our new faith begins to falter a bit. What we once easily accepted in light of our total depravity, now doesn't make sense, usually because we don't see how out present challenge is warranted in light of God's redemptive work in our life. And thus we encounter a minor (or major0 crisis of faith.

I have always compared this experience to that of a small child jumping to a father from the side of the pool. The child is aware he or she cannot swim and aware the water is deep. The child wants to jump for the thrill but isn't sure if father will catch them. But then finally, under the persistent persuasion of their father the child jumps, and the father does catches them. He or she is comfortable with the leap when the father is near to the edge of the pool and near to them. But as the father steps back, and back, and even further back there are questions. The child trusts easily when the father is nearby. As he steps away, the questions begin, even though he is the same father with the same knowledge and strength.

This is much like the experience of a crisis in a follower's life. During these times the leap of faith will be greater. And at this moment, we need to remember our Heavenly Father is the exactly the same. As the leap of faith becomes greater and presents new challenges, this does not mean our Father has changed. Just that the leap is more significant which gives us opportunity for a greater leap into the same Father's arms.

One timeless lesson we learn from Job is that we all will face a crisis of faith, one that will put our trust in God's sovereignty to the test. As we stand at the edge of this test, we may experience a wide array of emotions. Some so powerful that they will alter our feelings, persuade our thoughts, and change our actions. We have to keep in mind that Satan wants to persuade us toward disbelief. He will use any natural means possible. He will take our power, possessions, and people from us. He will use the counsel of people that care about us. And sometimes we are going to have fight through the fear, concerns, and questions that challenge our certainty of God's sovereignty. We are going to have to lean on that certainty of our first belief by believing above all uncertainty that God is still the same Father even though the leap of faith has changed. And in the end, if we continue to jump, we get a new experience in the divine catch of God's sovereign strength.

So in your crisis, you need to remember to fight for the belief that God is still sovereign. And this is not the power of positive thinking. This is the power we discover in the belief of the divine truth that God will never change even when our circumstances do.

QUESTION TWO | IN MY CRISIS, DID I DO SOMETHING TO DESERVE THIS?

In Job 7:20, Job says:

If I sin, what do I do to you, you watcher of mankind?
Why have you made me your mark?
Why have I become a burden to you?

JOB 7:20

I cannot tell you how many times I have felt this way in my life.

When we are suffering through a challenge we will look for that connection between our suffering and some specific sin in our life for which God is punishing us. And yes, sometimes our human suffering can be directly connected to a specific sin. For example, if I speed, I get a ticket, so I suffer through the embarrassment of getting pulled over, paying retribution, and the increases in my auto insurance premiums. The connection is easily made. But there are also times I go through seasons of suffering that a connection is not easily made. In an effort to end the suffering, I look for some cause-and-effect relationship so I can put a stop to it or make retribution that might end it. But sometimes that connection is not easily made. Maybe because it's not there.

We learn from the story of Job that sometimes suffering has no connection to a personal act of sin. In Job's case the suffering was initiated by Satan. You see, Satan was allowed to roam the earth and in doing so he incited confusion about God so that mankind would sin. Or that sometimes man would make connections to sin, where there was no sin, so that they would sin. Did you catch that? Sometimes in making a wrong connection to sin, where there is no sin, we end up sinning. And this is exactly what happens in the book of Job.

Let me illustrate. Job's three friends show up. They work hard to get Job to make an incorrect cause-and-effect connection between suffering and sin. Job has not sinned to deserve the suffering. So they add in a lot of confusion about how God works and they just won't let it go. In their mind, Job deserves the suffering. In Job's mind, he is certain he does not and he's okay with this, which is the right response. But these three friends double and triple down on the fact that Job needs to repent. They have drawn a connection that is not there. And they do so for two reasons. First, they misunderstand the sovereignty of God. And second, they are unaware the conversation in the heavenlies between God and Satan. Why do they work so hard to make this connection? They insist on a connection to some sin in Job's life.

The simple answer is that when God does not work in a way we like, we look to make God what we like. And most of the time we end up reducing God to our terms. Remember what I said last time? When we don't understand our suffering, we will reduce God's sovereignty to manageable terms to let him off the hook for sin and suffering. Therefore, our understandings of sin, suffering, justice, retribution, and blessing change because we have constructed a God of our making.

This is exactly what happens throughout the discussion with Job and his three friends. It's very subtle, so let me step you through it. Satan attempts to sway Job toward disbelief. He fails twice. Job still doesn't sin. So three friends come to mourn and minister to him. Out of genuine concern for Job, they try to help him find a path to end his suffering. They hold to a theory. It's only a theory. They assume a connection between his suffering and some personal sin. They look for a cause-and-effect relationship in the suffering. It's done in a genuine effort to help. However, in this case, there is no such connection. Job has not sinned. But the three friends don't believe it, so they persist by coming at Job with all kind evidence to prove their theory. They do this because they understand a God who punishes the disobedient and rewards the righteous — which is a rather small view of God. It's small because, they don't see that there is more to the story going on in the heavenlies. They are not privy to the debates between God and Satan. Therefore they reduce God to terms they can understand, given the evidence they have. God becomes someone they can understand. A God who does what they want. It's prosperity for the righteous. It's retribution for the disobedient. Its religion reduced to works-based righteous. A righteousness that we can achieve on our own, by our own effort — which is the most devious form of corrupt belief that elevates man against God. And notice, while we think Satan is done, he is not. He is using genuine friends, and genuine aid, to lead Job toward a genuinely wrong conclusion about God.

So from Job we discover the answer to our problematic question, "Did I do something to deserve this suffering?" And the answer is sometimes — no, you did nothing. Sometimes we will suffer, and it will have no connection to personal sin. This doesn't mean we shouldn't search our heart. We should search our heart. But if there is no connection, we should look right in the eye of suffering and continue to trust that something greater is going on in the heavenlies. We should leap into God's sovereign arms repeatedly.

Just to spoil the whole story, Satan used three friends to make a wrong connection in Job's life that ended up agitating Job just enough that Job does end up sinning. That's what happens when Job's righteousness turns into self-righteousness, all because his three friends make the wrong connection and kept beating on this man with his need for repentance. They make a man sin, the one who had not sinned, because they made a wrong connection to sin.

QUESTION THREE | IN MY CRISIS, WHY IS GOD SO FAR FROM ME?

In Job 23:8-10, Job says:

> *Behold, I go forward, but he is not there,*
> *and backward, but I do not perceive him;*
> *on the left hand when he is working, I do not behold him;*
> *he turns to the right hand, but I do not see him.*
> *But he knows the way that I take;*
> *when he has tried me, I shall come out as gold.*
>
> **JOB 23:8-10**

In crisis, I think we often we feel confused about God. We will sometimes describe this as feeling *"far"* from God. But this feeling is that it could not be further from the truth. Jesus, in John 14, was aware that after his departure that we would have these feelings. That our *"hearts would be troubled"* (John 14:1). And in anticipation of this he left us with *"the Helper, the Holy Spirit"* that the Father sent to us (John 14:26). We can conclude, actually, that we are not far from God at all. In fact, we are very close to God all the time, indwelled by the very Spirit of God living in us.

What we are confused about is not how *"far"* or *"close"* God is but rather how God is working in our present situation. Because in seasons of crisis God is not working in the ways we anticipate. We may not realize it, but throughout the course of our lives when we are not going through a crisis, we make these frequent cause-and-effect connections to what God is doing. We do this more than we think. And these connections become evidence for God. Sometimes these connections are wrong, and we make these very subtle deductions about how God works. We deduce that God is *"close"* to us when things are going well. But then crisis happens and all of sudden he is *"far"* from us. When really God is not close and far, he is just not playing by our assumptive rules.

What I love about what Job says is that he recognizes something wonderful in his own crisis. It's that while he may feel *"far"* from God he knows God will reveal the purpose in his pain. He knows that God is refining him like gold. And while he may not fully understand what God is doing at the present (since there is no cause-and-effect connection to a personal sin) he knows that God has a perspective on the situation that's far above his. He knows that while he cannot understand God, and may feel *"far,"* that God is not *"far."* God is just stirring and heating him in a cauldron, purifying him with purpose. This is very important. While we may not deserve a season of suffering, there is **no such thing as purposeless suffering for the Christian man**. We have to remember that God is sovereign over all things, including Satan, sin, and suffering. God knows our human limits. And God will raise a follower out of suffering better than he was before. He will even use senseless satanic suffering for redemptive purposes in our life. That's power!

We need to cling to this when we feel far from God. We need to remind ourselves that God is never far; He lives within us. In the end God will stretch our small understandings of him using undeserved suffering in our lives to show us how great and powerful a Redeemer he is.

If you are currently suffering. Continue to leap into the arms of a loving Father, even when you feel *"far"* you can know he is close. His Spirit dwells in you. And know that God is sovereign over your suffering. He will redeem you and refine you.

REFLECTION & DISCUSSION QUESTIONS:

- How did you question God's sovereignty in the crisis you mentioned previously?
- Did you ever identify some event or issue that led to your crisis of suffering?
- Did you ever feel "far" from God in that suffering?
- What did you learn from the book of Job that will strengthen you for the next crisis you may face?

THREE QUESTIONS WE ASK WHEN WE GO THROUGH A CRISIS

DEVOTIONALS FOR JOB 3-13

SO YOU HAD A BAD DAY

*After this Job opened his mouth
and cursed the day of his birth.*

JOB 3:1

I want to say how grateful I am for Job. I think this man is exceptional. I cannot wait to meet him in eternity. He endured events that I am not sure I would ever be able to endure. Nor would I wish these events even on an enemy. Job lost just about everything. And I mean everything: cattle, servants, land, and family. He suffered horrific boils all over his body. He had a wife who wanted him to give up, and he had three close friends who said some pretty damning things to him. Satan had been relentless. I would assume Job felt pretty lonely.

In chapter three Job lets us know how lonely he is. He sings a sad song. And I am so glad he does. He needs to break the silence. He needs to cry out. But there is something noticeable about chapter three. Job never curses God. He curses the day he was born, but never God. Even in the loneliness on the brink of death and excruciating pain, this man will not quit. He will not give up. He will not give in. He sings a sad song and hopes his life will end. But death never comes.

But hang on. Do you realize that in just one more long day, after forty chapters of long dialogue, Job is going to have the most brilliant day ever. Just one day after singing this song, he's going to talk with God face to face.

So if you are having a bad day and feeling lonely, try this: have faith in God by hanging on one more day. You too may have a brilliant day. God may show up and do something wonderful.

ASK THIS: Are you singing a sad song today?

DO THIS: Hang on one more day!

PRAY THIS: God, help me to hang on one more day!

THREE QUESTIONS WE ASK WHEN WE GO THROUGH A CRISIS

WHEN GOD IS BIGGER THAN BAD THEOLOGY

Remember: who that was innocent ever perished? Or where were the upright cut off?.

JOB 4:7

Over the next 38 chapters (which occur over one 24-hour period) we will hear a lot from Job's three friends. Eliphaz is the first to speak, and he will speak three different times. His counsel to Job is essentially found in this one verse. His point is that he cannot reconcile the suffering of a righteous man. It just doesn't fit into his theological understanding of God. To him, no innocent man or upright person would ever be cut off from natural blessings. He concludes that unrighteous men are cursed and righteous men are blessed. Therefore, as a result, he starts to formulate his position that Job's situation is certainly the result of some wrongdoing Job has done, which requires repentance.

Honestly, I am not sure I could look Job in the eye and even suggest something like this. Imagine turning to a father who has just lost everything, including ten children, and who is now writhing in pain from boils, saying, "Certainly this is your fault. Repent and return to God!"

We should know that righteous people are not excluded from suffering. The prime case in point is Jesus Christ. He was perfectly righteous and suffered wrong. So we can pitch the idea that righteous people don't suffer. Everyone suffers, even the righteous man.

But there is a bigger application here. Sometimes in suffering, we mistakenly misrepresent God. We put our theological foot in our mouth. We do this by suggesting reasons for another person's suffering. Occasionally this backfires and leads a suffering person further from God rather than closer to Him. Toward the end of this day, we will discover that in suffering, God reveals himself and he does not need our help. He is the Savior and we are not. We will also discover that we may not be able to reason with God at all.

In the end, here is what suffering people need: presence and prayer, not more bad theology.

ASK THIS: Who do you know that is suffering?

DO THIS: Call them and pray for them today, but don't preach!

PRAY THIS: God, help me to serve _____ today.

THE LIE OF SELF-RIGHTEOUSNESS

> *If I sin, what do I do to you, you watcher of mankind?*
> *Why have you made me your mark?*
> *Why have I become a burden to you?*
>
> **JOB 7:20**

So now we get to hear Job's first response to his three friends. Keep in mind the dialogue between Job and his friends will go back and forth a while, and I will only highlight a few comments from each of these men. This verse is fascinating because we get to hear Job respond to what he's thinking about Eliphaz's first remarks. Remember: Eliphaz suggested that Job needs to repent of his sin.

In the greater context of Job's response, we see that Job is simply commenting about his experiences and the challenges. But here it appears he momentarily turns to pose a question to God. We might imagine he looks up to the heavens and asks, "God, what did I do to you to deserve this?" And in this statement, we catch a subtle glimpse of self-justification. It's as if Job is looking for proof of his sin. But what's ironic is that in asking the question, he takes a step toward self-righteousness.

Self-righteousness is this. It's the idea that we are morally right and righteous of our own doing. And thus, when we come to this conclusion (that we are a right man in right standing) we believe we deserve certain rights. But this is a lie. It's a corrupt manner of thinking. There is no one who is right or righteous by his own doing. The problem here is that Eliphaz has seeded this thought with his corrupt theology suggesting righteous people don't suffer, which supports a theology of self-righteousness. Now it appears Job justifies himself in response to this idea, which results in the same corrupt end: a self-righteous questioning of God. The reason I take note of this is that self-righteousness is an insidious move toward self and away from God. Mature forms of self-righteousness lead to all kinds of hypocrisy and have a damaging effect on others hearing a gospel of grace.

C.S. Lewis once said this, *"A cold, self-righteous prig who goes regularly to church may be far nearer to hell than a prostitute."*

But self-righteousness is a challenge for everyone all the time. It can be challenging when times are good or times are bad. And the best thing for us to do when self-righteous thoughts occur is sacrifice them. Sacrifice them to our righteous God. For as soon as we think *"I deserve this"* or *"I don't deserve that,"* we've probably taken a step toward self-righteousness, and we need to correct our thinking before we become, as Lewis said, *"cold, self-righteous prigs."*

So today, will you join me in sacrificing any self-righteous thoughts, motives, or actions by getting right with a righteous God?

ASK THIS: What self-righteous thoughts, motives, and actions do you need to sacrifice to God?

DO THIS: Go low before God by giving him your self-righteousness.

PRAY THIS: God, forgive me for my self-righteousness.

WHEN WE ASSUME | RETRIBUTION THEOLOGY

*If your children have sinned against him,
he has delivered them into the hand of their
transgression.*

JOB 8:4

So now we move to the counsel of Job's next friend. His name is Bildad. And after reading this verse, I bet you wonder if Bildad is really a friend.

Here are three things we notice about Bildad and his position. First, he will build upon the opinion Eliphaz supports, which is that "righteous people don't suffer." Second, he is far less sympathetic to Job than Eliphaz. Third, he's way more direct in how he states things. Bildad's point of view is that God punished his children for their sin and is now punishing Job for his sin, and that Job needs to repent so that God will save him and restore his previous blessing.

His conclusion is, of course, wrong.

The theological name given to this position is Retribution Theology. It's the belief that one gets what one deserves. Think of it like Christian karma. It presumes a connection between good people and good things and bad people and bad things. Thus, this type of theology concludes that God rewards good people with good things and punishes bad people with bad things in this life. For example, if you contract a disease it's an indication that God is punishing you for something bad you've done. On the other hand, if you become wealthy in this life, it's an indication that God is blessing you for the good things you have done.

But there are all kinds of problems with applying this understanding of Retributive Theology and justice to the good and bad things that happen to us in this life. One problem is that bad things happen to good people. This is the lesson of Job's life. This was also the lesson of Christ's life. And sometimes this is the lesson of our life. Sometimes bad things happen to all people.

In fact, at the end of this life, there will be retributive justice, and it comes with some very bad news. It's found in Roman 3:23, which reads, "All have sinned and fall short of the glory of God." In other words, at the end of this life, we will all pay retribution for our sin because we are all sinful and fall short. The very wrong assumption of retributive theology is that we can be good enough to earn or deserve a blessing from God in this life and thus at the end of this life. This is just not possible. The only thing we deserve or earn is punishment for our sin. Even Job is not going to be able to earn his way back to a blessing from God.

But here is the good news: Jesus Christ paid the penalty for our sin, buying us back from the retribution we deserve at the end of this life. Because eventually, at the end of this life, there will be retribution for wrongdoing. God will both punish sin and reward righteousness. But his retribution for sin was paid for in the death and resurrection of Jesus Christ. In the end, we are all sinners who need redemption by God, who was willing to pay our retribution for sin so we can spend eternity with him. Now that's good news.

Today God will redeem you from the retribution you deserve. The Bible says, *"if you confess with your mouth that Jesus is Lord and believe in your heart that God raised him from the dead, you will be saved."* (Romans 10:9).

ASK THIS: Do you need to be bought back from your sin?

DO THIS: Let someone pray for you today.

PRAY THIS: God, I need you to forgive me and buy me back.

THREE QUESTIONS WE ASK WHEN WE GO THROUGH A CRISIS

THE SLIPPERY SLIDE OF SELF-JUSTIFICATION

There is no arbiter between us,
who might lay his hand on us both.

JOB 9:33

In chapters 9-10 we read Job's second response. But instead of responding directly to Bildad, who has been quite harsh, it appears Job is now trying to figure out how he can plead his case to God. These two chapters are very poetic and may appear worshipful, yet it has subtle undertones of what we call "righteous indignation." Job is weighing the greatness of God against the smallness of creation and his own life. Thus as he speaks, he begins to make himself a little too big and God a little too small. He wants a courtroom meeting with God because he is looking to justify himself, and this is a dangerous move.

I discovered a long time ago that self-justification is often my first line of defense when I feel cornered. I turn to self-justification to preserve my position when others put me to the test. This happens mostly when I am tested by people who know me well and see this disconnect in my integrity. People like my spouse and my children point this out the most. Therefore when tested, I will sometimes become defensive and use self-justification to preserve myself. I fortify my position by explaining, defending, and justifying my actions.

But let's remember that Job has done nothing wrong in this context to deserve this suffering. Let's also remember that his friends are making this worse by demanding that he has done something wrong. Because Job does not see the connection between his suffering and righteousness he wants to prove these men wrong and vindicate himself. What's ironic is that in trying to justify himself, he is no longer justifying his righteousness to Eliphaz, Bildad, and Zophar. He is justifying himself to God. He is asking for God to justify him before his friends so he can prove them wrong. And thus he has pushed too far. Satan has him. He is now elevating his righteousness and thus himself a little too much. We learn from Job that even when we are right, we can handle it wrong.

Do you see the slippery slide of self-justification? You know we all have moments like this. Moments we feel cornered. Moments we feel overwhelmed. Moments we feel trapped. And thus, we end up relying too much on ourselves and not enough on God. We self-preserve using self-justification because we trust ourselves and our own understanding more than we trust God. And thus we fall into the devious trap of Satan.

For those of you struggling with this today, here are some words for you to hold to from Proverbs 3:5-6:

THREE QUESTIONS WE ASK WHEN WE GO THROUGH A CRISIS

Trust in the Lord with all your heart,
and do not lean on your own understanding.
In all your ways acknowledge him,
and he will make straight your paths.

PROVERBS 3:5-6

ASK THIS: Have you fallen into the trap of self-justification lately?

DO THIS: Rectify it first with God and then with others.

PRAY THIS: God, forgive me for justifying myself to others and to you.

OTHERS WILL SOMETIMES JUMP TO CONCLUSIONS ABOUT YOU

*For you say, "My doctrine is pure,
and I am clean in God's eyes."*

JOB 11:4

In chapter 11, the last of Job's three friends gets his turn to offer counsel. His name is Zophar. Zophar declares an outright lie. He claims that Job has declared he's sinless. But Job has never even hinted at this. In fact, the only thing Job has declared is that he has done nothing wrong deserving of his present suffering. (And we know Job is right and Zophar is wrong.)

I have had a few moments like this in my life. Moments, for example, when a person made a statement about me that was untrue. Where someone jumped to a conclusion based on a false hypothesis and then declared this untruth to others. There were even a couple of times that this untruth had a long-standing effect on my life. It hurt. It resulted in wounding and scaring that took a long time to heal. And given all the suffering Job has endured, this adds insult to his injuries. He has to feel abandoned by friends who have come to the wrong conclusions, who are now attacking his integrity with their inaccurate assessments.

But we all jump to conclusions. What's so horrible about wrong conclusions is they can spread untruths about the identity of others. So today, give attention to your conclusions. Make sure and test them against what is true. If you have drawn some wrong conclusions about someone, go and rectify them. Free someone today from the bondage of your wrong conclusions. It may be good news that they need to hear.

ASK THIS: Do you need to free someone from your wrong conclusions? If so, what do you need to do to make this right?

DO THIS: Make it right.

PRAY THIS: God, forgive me for my wrong conclusions, and free others from my untrue beliefs and propaganda.

A RIGHTEOUS COMEBACK

Hear now my argument
and listen to the pleadings of my lips.
Will you speak falsely for God
and speak deceitfully for him?
Will you show partiality toward him?
Will you plead the case for God?
Will it be well with you when he searches you out?
Or can you deceive him, as one deceives a man?
He will surely rebuke you
if in secret you show partiality.
Will not his majesty terrify you,
and the dread of him fall upon you?
Your maxims are proverbs of ashes;
your defenses are defenses of clay.

JOB 13:6-12

I love an underdog, and Job is a total underdog. Please remember, Satan has come after Job. Robbers have come after Job. Natural disasters have come after Job. And now three friends, who should be more supportive have come after Job with a theological talk-down. Keep in mind; Job is still covered in painful oozing worm-filled boils. And somehow, he has been lucid enough to listen to these three men bloviate and respond with a righteous comeback.

THREE QUESTIONS WE ASK WHEN WE GO THROUGH A CRISIS

You know Job's endurance really makes me assess my own endurance. It forces me to access how willing I would be to suffer as Job suffered. In his statement here I think we discover the secret to his endurance. We see his endurance is the result of his undying devotion to the terrifying majesty of an Almighty God.

You know if you need to build endurance today. It's not manufactured from human strength. It's not manufactured by increased intensity, surviving more pain, or developing some mind-over-matter mindset. There is no amount of human effort or tactics that will help you build enough spiritual endurance to overcome spiritual challenges the way Job did. The only way to build spiritual endurance is with the Spirit's help by focusing relentlessly on the terrifying majesty of Almighty God. Because when all you fear is God, you will fear nothing you encounter in the flesh, and this results in endurance.

ASK THIS: Do you need endurance for your present season?

DO THIS: Fear God more than you present circumstance.

PRAY THIS: God, I believe that you are trying to teach me to trust in you more than the circumstances of this life. Increase my trust, faith, and fear of you.

HOW TO SPEAK UP WHEN IT'S OUR PLACE TO SPEAK UP

OPENING QUESTIONS:
- Have you ever been silent when you should have spoken up?
- Have you ever spoken up when you should have been silent?
- What do you wish you would have done in each of the situations?

LESSON 4

There is a lot happening in the world today. And because there is so much happening, we can feel confused and frustrated. For many of us we feel compelled to speak up. I know I do. But the challenge is knowing how and when to speak.

As I have reflected on this conundrum, I've remembered many moments throughout my life where I was unsure if I was supposed to speak up or not. This happened in my teens, through college, in my career, and even in my marriage. I encountered moments where I was unsure if I supposed to open my mouth or keep it shut.

But after a quick assessment I think we all soon discover that there is regret on either side of this issue. Because there have been moments I have **not spoken up** that I regretted **not saying something**. And there have also been moments I have **spoken up** that I regretted **saying something**. I have lived long enough now to experience both sides of this regret. Many times. But I have learned one thing from this experience in my life. That it's *never* perfectly safe to speak. Nor is it perfectly safe to *not* speak.

It dangerous and risky on both sides of the conundrum. At some point, we simply have to say something. And by saying something we are attempting to create order in chaos by speaking truth into the situation. So the only conclusion I can come to is when I speak up I am always taking a risk.

In this section we are going to look a young man who takes a risk. A big one.

Here's the situation: Job has been speaking with three older men who were friends. This has cycled to an end and then we find that there was another man listening in. A fifth man. He is much younger than the other men. His name is Elihu and he finally speaks up, mostly because he is irritated with all of them. In fact, of everyone who speaks in Job, Elihu speaks the most. He speaks even more than Job and God. His material consumes six very long chapters and it's quite spectacular how he builds his case. It's so good that God never condemns his speech. But what I found very interesting about these six chapters is how Elihu addressed the issue. It was not just what he said, but how he did it that was interesting. In a very tense situation, Elihu handled the matter very well, and he spoke up in a way that teaches us four things about speaking up when a situation demands we do so.

Let's look at four sections in these six chapters and learn how to speak up when it's our time to do so:

First, if a situation demands you speak...

First | Check Your Emotional Dashboard Before You Speak

Consider two parts of Job 32: Job 32:6 and 32:18-22. Listen to Elihu:

> *I am young in years,*
> *and you are aged;*
> *therefore I was timid and afraid*
> *to declare my opinion to you.*
>
> **JOB 32:6**

> *For I am full of words;*
> *the spirit within me constrains me.*
> *Behold, my belly is like wine that has no vent;*
> *like new wineskins ready to burst.*
> *I must speak, that I may find relief;*
> *I must open my lips and answer.*
> *I will not show partiality to any man*
> *or use flattery toward any person.*
> *For I do not know how to flatter,*
> *else my Maker would soon take me away.*
>
> **JOB 32:18-22**

As Christians we do have a responsibility to speak up. But how we speak up matters. Elihu sets a good example as a younger man. He goes directly to the party and offers some feedback. And there are three actions he takes that I think are commendable. First, he is open about how he feels because he is aware that something isn't right within him. I'm not exactly sure how you might categorize his feelings here, maybe frustration or anger, but he is enough in touch with his feelings enough that he can regulate them and share them accurately. He shares them in a very vulnerable manner. Second, he shares his concerns about sharing. This is also commendable since it signals to his audience that he is about to give feedback that he has some level of discomfort about. Third, he tries to be impartial in his feedback. I think based on the chapters of material we can read from Elihu, he really tries to be objective even though he is very passionate. He attempts to identify the root problem and works hard to not assign blame where there is no blame, thus distracting from the core issues. And honestly, he does such a good job that God never corrects him.

These are three awesome steps. Let me restate them. First, being open about how we feel. Second, sharing genuine concerns. Third, focusing on being impartial. But my problem is remembering to do these things when I need to use them the most. If I could just remember to do these things when things get heated. Man, I would act a lot more like Elihu.

There is one thing that we can do to help us remember. It helps me to take the right first step. It's this: it's becoming more aware of how we feel. For example, when we encounter moments that elicit frustration or anger, we must choose to listen to our feelings. Feelings function a lot like the indicator lights on the dashboard on our car. They tell us when something isn't functioning right. They alert us. Rather than ignoring our feelings or just speaking and acting, we should listen to our feelings because they are indicating something. I have discovered I am much better at responding to people when I recognize my emotional dashboard is lit up and alerting me that something that isn't right. So I pull myself to the side of the road and I do a couple of things. One, I assess what I am feeling. Two, I assess why I am feeling it. And once I have a handle on the feelings and the reasons, then I respond. All this can happen in the confines of our mind within a few moments. Simply by taking the first step of becoming more aware of how I feel, I have found I respond better. In fact, when I am aware that my emotional dashboard is lit up, I respond to everyone better. I respond better to my wife in moments of tension, better to my boss when frustrated, better to my children when they're disobedient, and better to the car in front of me that just cut me off. But it all starts with awareness.

But still in life there are these moments we are caught off-guard. They happen to everyone. They are moments that we might be caught off-guard and don't yet know how we feel. I believe there is nothing wrong with signaling to another person by saying something one of these three things:

- *I am not sure if I am ready to respond.*
- *I need some time to process what I just heard.*
- *I can answer if you like, but I need to assess how I feel for a minute.*

You know what? We are never going to be perfect, but we can take one step at a time and mature through these experiences like Elihu demonstrates for us here. So, the next time a situation demands you speak. Check your emotional dashboard first. Then, when you have assessed what you feel and why you feel that way, speak up and be vulnerable.

Second, if a situation demands you speak...

SECOND | SPEAK FOR THEIR BENEFIT

Next let's skip forward to Job 33, where Elihu corrects Job for some things he has said. Here are some statements found in Job 33:9, 12, and 32-33:

You say, 'I am pure, without transgression;
I am clean, and there is no iniquity in me.

JOB 33:9

Behold, in this you are not right. I will answer you,
for God is greater than man.

JOB 33:12

If you have any words, answer me;
speak, for I desire to justify you.
If not, listen to me;
be silent, and I will teach you wisdom.

JOB 33:32-33

In these three statements Elihu declares his rebuttal process. First, he restates something Job has said. Second, he explains how this is wrong. Third (and I think this is important) he explains that he is correcting Job for Job's benefit. He wants to *"justify"* him and see him in right standing before God. And Elihu engages these three steps a few times in his long dissertation. But it's this last step I think is intriguing.

I think most of the time when we are being given feedback by another person we don't realize the other person is trying to help us. We become emotionally hooked, so we focus on the hurtful things being said and miss the help they are trying to provide.

I will admit that I used to perceive all feedback negatively—even feedback that was delivered appropriately. When someone gave me feedback, I focused on things like:

1. *The negative way the feedback was being delivered.*
2. *The negative traits of the person delivering it.*
3. *What I had done wrong that led to the feedback.*
4. *The hurt I had inflicted on someone else that resulted in the need to give it in the first place.*

This is a pretty defeating list of things to focus on. I was so focused on these things that every presentation of feedback became this difficult and negative experience for me. Eventually I had to address this. I had to unlearn thinking this way and start listening to people differently. The one thing that helped me delete all these negative scripts and write new ones was a few short words I would speak silently to myself. When someone was giving me feedback, I would say these words in my mind. *"Remember, God is trying to help you."* It's a very simple script. I sometimes call this rescripting *"preaching to myself."* By doing this over and over I wrote a new script in my mind when people gave me feedback. I also discovered that during feedback sessions most people were seeking to help me just as Elihu was with Job. Over time I came to discover that all feedback, even poorly conveyed feedback, delivered by people of extremely poor character was for my benefit; that God was always *"trying to help me"* in some way, even in ways sometimes that I didn't want to be helped.

So let's step back for a minute, because I want to look at this from the other angle. Not from the position of receiving feedback but from being the person who offers it.

Like Elihu, when we have an opportunity to give feedback and correct others of their wrongs it's important to focus on the benefit. The feedback Elihu offers is relatively simple. It's entirely for Job's benefit. Job is thinking too highly of himself. Elihu knows that the three friends have come to some wrong conclusions about God, which have led to some bad counsel, which have led to Job defend himself, thus he has elevated his righteousness a bit too much. Elihu corrects Job because he wants Job to stay low and God to stay high.

What Elihu models is practical and spiritual. If a situation demands that you speak, correct the wrong for the other person's benefit, not your own. Stay focused on this in hopes that they, too, will see that you care about them.

Third, if a situation demands you speak...

THIRD | SPEAK TO THE INJUSTICE

Here are a few verses from chapters 34 and 35:

> For Job has said, 'I am in the right,
> and God has taken away my right;
> in spite of my right I am counted a liar;
> my wound is incurable, though I am without transgression.'
>
> **JOB 34:5-6**

> Therefore, hear me, you men of understanding:
> far be it from God that he should do wickedness,
> and from the Almighty that he should do wrong.
>
> **JOB 34:10**

> Of a truth, God will not do wickedly,
> and the Almighty will not pervert justice.
>
> **JOB 34:12**

> *If you have sinned, what do you accomplish against him?*
> *And if your transgressions are multiplied, what do you do to him?*
>
> **JOB 35:6**

I am referencing these four sections because I want you to notice the logic presented by Elihu. It's a very cunning presentation, dismantling the broken logic of Job.

1. Man has done right, therefore...
2. God has done wrong, therefore...
3. God is unjust, therefore...(the conclusion)
4. Our sin affects God's justice.

This is a powerful use of logic by Elihu to dismantle Job's argument. He shows Job the natural conclusion of reasoning. Steps one, two, and three are what Job has already concluded. Let me restate them. *Man has done right. God has done wrong, God is unjust.* But Elihu shows him that he needs to think it through a little further, because he has not taken the final step in the progression of his logic. Step four. Job's logic concludes *our sin affects God's justice.* And we have all used the same logic Job does here. We do this all the time in human relationships. We conclude:

1. *I have done right.*
2. *They have done wrong.*
3. *They are unjust.*

Don't we do this?

I do; maybe you don't. I believe this is the basis for every human argument we have in life. But the problem here is that Job tries to use this logic to preserve himself before his friends and God. As Elihu points out, we cannot use this logic model with God because the correct logic model is:

1. *Man always does wrong.*
2. *God always does right.*
3. *God is always just.*
4. *Human sin never affects God's justice.*

Of all the things Elihu says, I think Job 35:6 is the ultimate haymaker for Job and the three friends. It destroys all their reasoning and foregone conclusions. Listen to this wisdom. He says:

> *If you have sinned, what do you accomplish against him?*
> *And if your transgressions are multiplied,*
> *what do you do to him?*
>
> **JOB 35:6**

The answer is: *nothing*. You do nothing to God. Sin does not affect God. Nor does our righteousness affect God. But notice this, and it's profound and yet so simple. Elihu makes this point using questions. Simple but profound questions. Both Job and the three friends have to consider the conclusions of their reasoning on their own. This is critical. The questions force both

Job and the three men to consider:

- Job is forced to consider that his **righteous acts** do not affect God.
- The three friends are forced to consider that **sinful acts** do not affect God.

This is so laser-sharp and cunning it blows my mind.

I think when a situation demands we speak, it is good to clarify the injustice. There will always be an injustice we want to address. And we should speak to it. But we should be able to identify the injustice and talk about it logically. Elihu models this. He is not just spouting off on social media or sending out a hateful email blast or canceling people for no reason. He is speaking intelligibly about the issue and encouraging his brothers to consider the unfortunate end of their logic using a couple of great questions.

Fourth, if a situation demands you speak...

FOUR | REMEMBER IT'S NOT ABOUT YOU

Listen to these final words in Job 36:22-23 by Elihu:

> *Behold, God is exalted in his power;*
> *who is a teacher like him?*
> *Who has prescribed for him his way,*
> *or who can say, 'You have done wrong'?*
>
> **JOB 36:22-23**

As Elihu concludes he leads us on this great ascent toward the Great Teacher. It's his reminder to us that God is the teacher, and we are students. Even as we read the New Testament, we discover that Jesus, the greatest teacher of all time, took his cues directly from God. Jesus as a student said this in John 12:49:

For I have not spoken on my own authority, but the Father who sent me has himself given me a commandment—what to say and what to speak.

Elihu echoes this same father-son and teacher-student relationship. He reminds us that man is merely a student of the one and only Teacher. If a situation demands we speak, we need to remind ourselves of this, that we don't speak up to make a point, but to point people to God.

We are not truth. Sometimes when we see a truth that someone else doesn't see we like to draw attention to the fact that we see something someone else doesn't see. This only pits us against another person by using the truth to draw attention to ourselves. But honestly the only truth we know in this life is God's truth. Truth only exists in this world because God made it known. And we never possess this. We only get to proclaim what God has already proclaimed. In fact, every time I preach or teach, I am reminded about this. When I teach my goal is not to show you how much I know. I didn't make this stuff up. I am not that smart. (Just ask my wife.) It's God's truth, I am just reiterating it in a way that makes it more contemporary. And when I get to heaven, I am pretty sure God is going to charge me with a massive plagiarism lawsuit! So my goal isn't to get you to fall in love with me, but fall in love with God the Creator of all Truth.

To conclude ,the simplest call to action would be this. Remember that when it's your turn to speak up it's not about you, it's all about God. When you open your mouth, you need to remember you are trying to direct people to God. To God's truth. To a relationship with God. It's not about you or me at all. It's always about him.

So there you have it. When you speak up, remember these four things that Elihu demonstrates for us here:

1. *Check your emotional dashboard.*
2. *Speak for their benefit.*
3. *Speak to the injustice.*
4. *Remember it's not about you.*

And as you do, let God speak his truth, in his way, and in his time.

REFLECTION & DISCUSSION QUESTIONS:

- Do you consistently check your emotions before you speak? Why or why not? What could you do differently?
- When you speak up are you focused on your injustice or their benefit?
- How can you stay focused on the injustice without eviscerating the person?

DEVOTIONALS FOR JOB 15-25

GOD IS BIGGER

> *Are you the first man who was born?*
> *Or were you brought forth before the hills?*
>
> **JOB 15:7**

Remember that each one of Job's friends gets a turn to counsel Job on the reason for his present suffering. In chapter 15 we begin round two with each of the three friends. We are back to the first of Job's friends, Eliphaz. Eliphaz is still convinced that Job is guilty of sin, which is the exclusive reason for his present suffering. But now, he will notch it up by proposing that Job's claim of suffering as righteous is preposterous. He claims this would be like comparing himself to the sinless state of Adam before the fall.

Here is an historical note. Based on the internal evidence found in the book of Job, we can conclude that Job is one of the earliest books in the entire Bible. Theologians believe, with high probability, that Moses wrote the book. He probably wrote it before he wrote the first five books of the Bible, what we commonly call the Pentateuch (i.e., Genesis, Exodus, Leviticus, Numbers, and Deuteronomy).

What's especially interesting is that Job and Moses lived after the flood. This is important because the flood was God's punishment for humanity's perpetual disobedience. What was once good in the garden was given over to increasing sin and selfishness. Therefore God destroyed life on the earth because he was grieved. He made man and saw that the intentions of man's heart was nothing but evil. But remember, God saved a few people: Noah and his family. Then from Noah's family a new genealogy originated, and Job was one of those descendants. So were Eliphaz, Bildad, and Zophar. I would assume that the flood and Adam's fall in the Garden were on their minds as they were contemplating the reason for Job's suffering. In the end, Job's friends have concluded that there is a cause-and-effect relationship between disobedience and God's punishment, as well as obedience and God's blessing. It would be easy to conclude this if you assume Noah's righteousness saved him. But Noah's righteousness did not save Noah and his family. It was God's favor, and this favor was evidenced by Noah's faith. For proof of this, turn to Genesis 6:8 and Hebrews 11:7. Note: Noah was a sinner, just like us. There was nothing righteous he could do to be saved. It was simply God's favor that saved him. God was about to destroy all mankind because all mankind grieved him.

I wonder if some of Eliphaz's theological misconceptions came from drawing this wrong connection. These three men picked up their corrupt reasoning somewhere, and they are using historical events as evidence for their position. Eliphaz does so here, reaching back to Adam in the garden, pre-fall. This is called deductive reasoning. Deductive reasoning is where we develop a hypothesis and look for evidence to prove the point. But their reasoning has resulted in them bending the truth in a direction that suits them. And why do they do this? Because we all want to believe that if we do what is right and righteous we will receive a blessing. We all want to believe that if we attend to our marriages righteously, raise our kids to honor God, work ethically in a way that pleases the Lord, and love our neighbors everything will work out for us, and God will bless us. But that's not the case. You know that's not the case. And what we learn from these three men here is that when our reasoning is corrupted by selfish tendencies, we will find ways to mold God to our views and our ways.

> *Left to ourselves, we tend immediately to reduce God to manageable terms.*
>
> **AW TOZER.**

Tozer's point is when left to ourselves, using deductive reasoning, we will find ways to make God smaller and us bigger. And this is what Eliphaz is doing. He is using biblical events to prove his selfish hypothesis.

Where in your mind do you try to get God to behave in a way that fits what you hope he will do, so he will be who you hope he will be? We all do this in one way or another. We do this in our marriages when we hope our spouses will feel, think, and act a certain way and ask God to do this for us. We do the same with our children and hope God will help them turn out the way we want them to turn out and even pray that God will do this for us. We do this with our dreams and careers, hoping God will point us down a specific direction or help us achieve something we have conceived in our minds?

But however you do it, just *stop* doing it. Let God be God. Let him be even bigger than how you want him to behave and what you hope he will do. Bring your requests to him with no expectations. When he answers, accept it. And don't try to make a connection to something you did only to rob glory from something great God has done.

ASK THIS: Where in your mind do you try to get God to behave in a way that fits what you hope he will do so he will be who you hope he will be?

DO THIS: Present the person or issue to God and leave it with him.

PRAY THIS: God, you are awesome. Be awesome. Act awesome. And whatever you do, do it for your glory. Not mine. I love you.

STOP BEING A BLOWHARD

> *Then Job answered and said:*
> *"I have heard many such things;*
> *miserable comforters are you all.*
> *Shall windy words have an end?*
> *Or what provokes you that you answer?"*
>
> **JOB 16:1-3**

These words are laughable. The biting sarcasm of Job here is honest, transparent, and real. In fact, as an actionable item today you need to read chapters 16-17. I want to especially encourage you to do this if you are suffering right now. You might find this kindred connection with Job. Even try to read these two chapters out loud. As you do, you will hear Job move through this progressive state of despair. First, he snaps back at his friends. Second, he proclaims that God is targeting him with their counsel. Third, we hear him hit the point where his spirit is broken. Fourth, he is so exhausted he longs to be set free by death.

You know we will all go through moments of despair in our lives. But here is what I don't get. I don't understand why these men do this to him. I have seen this happen so many times: where those who fear God sometimes shoot wounded. But I know why they do it. They think they have God figured out. And a person who thinks they have God figured out tends to "solve" rather than support, and "teach" rather than comfort. I have done this so many times. When my wife has a bad day, I try to solve rather than support her. When my children make a mistake, I teach rather than comfort them. There is a time for teaching and solving, but sometimes a hurting person only needs support because the situation is doing the teaching. Besides, support and comfort are rich with theology, and they tend to do less harm to a hurting person. So the next time you are near someone who is hurting consider this: stop being a blowhard.

ASK THIS: Who is hurting around you that needs your comfort?

DO THIS: Read Job 16-17 out loud today.

PRAY THIS: God, bring comfort to those who are hurting. And may I be a minister of your grace to someone today.

A SHOUT OF ENCOURAGEMENT

> *He breaks me down on every side, and I am gone,*
> *and my hope has he pulled up like a tree.*
> *He has kindled his wrath against me*
> *and counts me as his adversary.*
>
> **JOB 19:10-11**

There will be moments in our life that we will feel alone. Abandoned by people and by God. This is a terrible feeling. It's one that Job describes well. One where we feel detached from resources and in this losing battle with God.

But here's the good news. While we've been reading through Job now for days, all these conversations with Job happened in only one day. It takes place over just hours in this one day, after a few conversations with some heartless friends that Job begins to lose heart. And yet we all know because we can read ahead in the story that the end of this day will be incredible.

As a spectator to Job's despair, I want to shout to him from the sidelines.

"Hold on, Job. Hold on. Don't give in. Don't say anything stupid. Don't listen to those fools. Don't give up. Hang on, just a few more hours. The end is coming! It's going to be marvelous."

Today, I want you to consider one person who needs to hear a shout of encouragement, a person who is down and almost out. Shoot them a text. Send them an email. Give them a call. Then speak a message of hope to them as they feel uprooted and surrounded. Together may our shouts echo across time to those who feel abandoned about a God who never, never, never, never, never, ever abandons anyone.

Be strong and courageous. Do not fear or be in dread of them, for it is the Lord your God who goes with you. He will not leave you or forsake you.

DEUTERONOMY 31:6

ASK THIS: Who needs a shout of encouragement from you?

DO THIS: Tell them today. Don't wait.

PRAY THIS: God, I want to pray for those who feel abandoned today. Will you please be their comfort. And may my shouts of courage lift them up.

JOB

WHEN WICKED PEOPLE PROSPER

Why do the wicked live,
reach old age, and grow mighty in power?
Their offspring are established in their presence,
and their descendants before their eyes.
Their houses are safe from fear,
and no rod of God is upon them.
Their bull breeds without fail;
their cow calves and does not miscarry.
They send out their little boys like a flock,
and their children dance.
They sing to the tambourine and the lyre
and rejoice to the sound of the pipe.
They spend their days in prosperity,
and in peace they go down to Sheol.
They say to God, 'Depart from us!
We do not desire the knowledge of your ways.
What is the Almighty, that we should serve him?
And what profit do we get if we pray to him?'
Behold, is not their prosperity in their hand?
The counsel of the wicked is far from me.

JOB 21:7-16

One of the major arguments of Job's friends is that righteous people don't suffer. They conclude that Job's suffering is a result of sin in his life, which requires repentance. And somehow, through this immense suffering and the belligerent counsel of these friends, Job is still lucid enough to bark back at this futile reasoning. He argues that if righteous people never suffer, as they suggest, then why are wicked people prospering. Which is a great point. You think this would completely dismantle their argument. But it doesn't.

In this life, the wicked and the righteous both suffer and prosper. Some righteous men are prosperous, and others live in poverty. Some wicked men are prosperous, and others live in poverty. One of Satan's great methods of deception is to get a righteous person to compare themselves with someone they know who is more prosperous. To compare our poverty to their prosperity and thus make a judgment about God's injustice to us. And when we fall for this deception, we will make this comparison, only to draw a conclusion that could be a tragic mistake.

I, too, at times, have done this. But I have learned to take this thought captive. With urgency, I must reject this deception. It is a Satanic illusion. I must immediately preach to myself when this thought comes to mind. *"Vince, your riches are not of this world."* This preaching is straight from the preaching of Jesus in the Sermon on the Mount. It is found in Matthew 6:19-20. I need to preach this to myself to take every thought captive. (see 2 Corinthians 10:5). Because I know this small thought will result in reasoning that elevates my ways and desires above God's ways and his desires.

So today, when the illusion presents itself and you feel this compulsion to compare yourself with someone else, preach to yourself.. Don't accept the illusion. It's only a deception. The good news is this: you are rich.

2 Corinthians 8:9 reads, *"For you know the grace of our Lord Jesus Christ, that though he was rich, yet for your sake he became poor, so that you by his poverty might become rich."*

ASK THIS: What wrong comparison have you made?

DO THIS: Preach to yourself.

PRAY THIS: God, may I move my eyes from my temporal poverty and from comparison to others to the eternal riches you have generously given me.

GREAT WORDS THAT REQUIRE GREAT COMMITMENT

> For I know that my Redeemer lives,
> and at the last he will stand upon the earth.
> And after my skin has been thus destroyed,
> yet in my flesh I shall see God,
> whom I shall see for myself,
> and my eyes shall behold, and not another.
> My heart faints within me!
>
> **JOB 19:25-27**

These are incredible words from Job. A man suffering like he is should not be able to speak them. But because he does, we see a collection of radical contrasts that inspire us to greater faith. Faith in the Spirit, and not the flesh. Faith in the future, and not the present. Faith in the unseen, and not the seen. Faith in a Redeemer who will redeem and not destroy.

While Job is a man marked by physical circumstances, his commitment will not be altered. He is committed to living by faith in a dying body. A faith determined to see God regardless of the pain that may come his way.

Are you this man?

ASK THIS: What issue(s) do you need to address to live all in for Him?

DO THIS: Share these issues with someone and ask for prayer.

PRAY THIS: God, may I die to self and live for you today.

I WILL RESURRECT LIKE REFINED GOLD

But he knows the way that I take;
when he has tried me, I shall come out as gold.

JOB 23:10

Job acknowledges three essential truths. First, Job acknowledges that God is still in control. He is aware in his suffering that Satan, sympathizers, and the situation will convince him that he is far from God. But Job is confident. God is not far but "knows the way Job takes." Second, Job acknowledges that the challenges of this season will eventually become something of the past. Notice his use of the past tense: "when God has tried me." Third, Job acknowledges a future benefit, and he is focused on this benefit. The present fire, while hot, also produces heat that refines. He knows that when God turns up the heat, he is refining. He has been chosen to become something better and of greater value. He is going to "come out as gold."

If you are going through a Job-like season, you will naturally believe:

- *That God is distant from you.*
- *That your trial has no end.*
- *That there is no purpose in your suffering.*

But these three assertions are not the truth. They are lies. The truth is what we hear Job preach to himself. What Job proclaims to friends that try to sway him to believe otherwise. They are:

- *That God is near and in control.*
- *That this trial will end.*
- *That there is purpose in this season that God will use to refine you and make you better.*

This is not the power of positive thinking. This is the power of an Almighty God refining you like precious, valuable gold. Hang on, brother. You will emerge like refined gold.

ASK THIS: Which of the three truths do you need to cling to today?

DO THIS: Believe this truth. Cast off the lie. And ask others to pray for increased belief.

PRAY THIS: God, help me to reject the lies of my mind and believe your truth. Strengthen my faith. I invite you to refine me.

WHEN STUPIDITY COMES TO AN END

> *Then Bildad the Shuhite answered and said:*
> *"Dominion and fear are with God;*
> *he makes peace in his high heaven.*
> *Is there any number to his armies?*
> *Upon whom does his light not arise?*
> *How then can man be in the right before God?*
> *How can he who is born of woman be pure?*
> *Behold, even the moon is not bright,*
> *and the stars are not pure in his eyes;*
> *how much less man, who is a maggot,*
> *and the son of man, who is a worm!"*
>
> **JOB 25:1-6**

This is the last time we hear from these friends. Thank God! If you have been reading through Job with me, you've seen that each of these three men speaks on a rotation. And each time, their bloviating gets shorter and shorter. This is because they are running out of things to say.

But these last few words from Bildad are very insightful. While he was wrong to assume that Job was suffering because of a specific sin, he is right about two claims he makes here. One is a claim about God, and one is a claim about man. Claim one: God is sovereign. He is sovereign over all things. Dominion and justice reside with him. Claim two: man is sinful; he is born and dies in this depraved state. While much of his counsel is wrong, Bildad's final claims are spot on.

Humanity is born sinful. This is a fact. We are selfish, and we reject God from our first breath to the last. The result of this depravity is spiritual death evidenced by physical death. For us to overcome this state of despair, we need to be rescued by God. Therefore God in his grace provides us with a second birth. A spiritual rebirth. in fact, Jesus taught that we could be "born again." (John 3:3) This second birth is where man ceases to be a child of man and becomes a child of God. And this second birth occurs at the moment we reject our old ways of leading our own life and let Jesus be the leader of our life. It says this in John 3:16.

For God so loved the world, that he gave his only Son, that whoever believes in him should not perish but have eternal life.

JOHN 3:16

Today may be a day you want to make that decision. You can do that right now. Believe in Jesus Christ. Reject your old life. Accept God's gift of new and eternal life by submitting to Jesus as your Lord and Savior. You can become a child of God today. If you made this decision today, let me know, and I will send some resources your way that may help you get started in those first steps of your new life.

ASK THIS: Are you ready to make Jesus your Lord and Savior and be born again? Or do you know someone who needs Jesus as their Lord and Savior?

DO THIS: Believe! Or ask God to help a person's unbelief.

PRAY THIS: God, I want to make you my Lord and Savior. And I know other people who may need to do the same.

GOD INTERROGATES JOB: FOUR LESSONS

OPENING QUESTIONS:

- How would you feel if God showed up and interrogated you?
- What do you think Job will learn from the experience?
- Have you ever had a moment in your life where God challenged you? Describe this moment, how you felt, and what you did.

LESSON 5

At the close of the Book of Job, we encounter an epic interaction of God with man. It's one of those moments we think we want to have with God, but when we have it, we discover we really didn't want it. Thankfully Job gets to experience it for all of us so we know what it's like.

Be sure to read this section of the text. It's basically God asking Job questions. It's very poetic, but I want to focus on time on four lessons we learn from God's interrogation of Job.

LESSON ONE | GOD IS UNLIMITED

God says to Job in 38:2-4:

> *"Who is this that darkens counsel by words without knowledge? Dress for action like a man; I will question you, and you make it known to me. "Where were you when I laid the foundation of the earth? Tell me, if you have understanding.*
>
> **JOB 38:2-4**

If you remember, the argument of Job centers around the topic of God's justice. Then God shows up in chapters 38-42 and he helps us all to understand that the debate and logic of Job and his friends is driven by one underlying (wrong) assumption. It's the assumption that a man within the limits of creation can understand the justice of a divine God. Now their debate may start with an attempt to understand the justice God, but the conversation cycles downward pitting their understanding of God's justice against a right understanding of God's justice. And God shows up to point out how injudicious their debate has become. He wants them to understand the injustice of their conclusions.

And really, God does this in a polite way. Now, we may not think about it as polite. Chapters 38-42 look like a talk down and an interrogation. But remember, God has the right to just strike them dead. He could. Instead, he is pressing Job to consider the assumptions and motives behind his debate. He does this by presenting Job with questions about creation. God dares him to answer just one of hundreds of questions about the origin and the organization of things within creation. And God knows that Job is unable to answer even one of them. Thus he is forcing him to think about his assumptions, logic, and conclusions.

So here's what God does. He presents Job with the enormity of his creation: the foundations of the earth, the depths of the sea, the source of light, the doors of death, the storerooms of the snow, the systems of stars, the intricacies of nature, and the mystery of the human heart. Essentially, he points to everything in creation and ask Job this question:

Since you know so much as a mere mortal man, tell me how these things work and how they came to pass?

But of course, Job cannot answer even one of these questions.

The point that God is making is that his ways, ability, thinking, and justice and have no comparison to ours. They are not even in the same solar system. In fact, God says if you are so great, make your own solar system.

We have an incredible unlimited God but mankind tends to limit God. Remember this from lesson one? This story is told repeatedly throughout the Bible. Almost every biblical story has a moment within it where we discover that man limits his understanding of God, and then God shows up and does something bigger and better than we expect. Just when we think something is impossible, God makes it possible. Yet what happens is we become convinced that this life and its circumstances re all we have. We become inundated with the natural and therefore miss the supernatural, and the result is the reduction of a limitless God.

We need to remember; the most worshipful moments of life are those where we come to realize the speck we are. We must remember that we have no control over the things of this life and that God is greater, and we are not.

LESSON TWO | MAN IS SMALL

Listen to Job's response to God in Job 40:3-5:

> *Then Job answered the Lord and said: "Behold, I am of small account; what shall I answer you? I lay my hand on my mouth. I have spoken once, and I will not answer; twice, but I will proceed no further."*
>
> **JOB 40:3-5**

So, this interrogation by God has led Job to discover something important. How *small* he is. This is a very important discovery because the truth about a man is that he likes to think *big* of himself. A man naturally thinks more of himself than he thinks about others. Thus, self-centeredness has been, is, and always will be our greatest challenge. Call it hubris, or pride, or arrogance, or self-centeredness but it always originates from the same issue: *thinking big of ourselves.*

In our world today we encourage and even endorse a *big* focus on self. Modern marketing trains us to feed on our selfish desires by purchasing and possessing. Social media trains us to feed on our selfish activities by posting and receiving rewards. In schools self-esteem is even taught as a phycological tactic to boost attention to the self when we feel down or defeated. All these systems, strategies, and tactics do is train us to think *big* of ourselves.

But in this interrogation by God, Job discovers something important that man needs to understand. That making ourselves *big* does not solve our problems. The solution is discovering our smallness in relationship to a big God. Or it might be better said, discovering our limits in relationship to a limitless God. It's discovering God is the Creator, and we are the creation, not a god. This is where man begins and ends.

I believe each man will eventually have a confrontation with the smallness of himself and the bigness of God. I did. I remember hitting what some call *rock-bottom* in my life and discovering that I could not make it out without divine intervention. Some discover this when they hit rock-bottom in their marriage, in their career, in an addiction, or in a health crisis. But eventually we must come to terms with the limits of our human bigness. It's at this point we all have carefrontation with God, much like Job does here. God confronts Job directly with how *big* he really is. And it leaves him speechless.

And what Job does here is commendable. He recognizes his smallness. But as we discover Job does not take this far enough. So God continues to interrogate Job till he responds to God's bigness. Which brings us to the final lesson from the interaction.

LESSON THREE | MAN'S RESPONSE

Listen to Job's response to God in Job 42:1-6:

Then Job answered the Lord and said: "I know that you can do all things, and that no purpose of yours can be thwarted. 'Who is this that hides counsel without knowledge?' Therefore I have uttered what I did not understand, things too wonderful for me, which I did not know. 'Hear, and I will speak; I will question you, and you make it known to me.' I had heard of you by the hearing of the ear, but now my eye sees you; therefore I despise myself, and repent in dust and ashes."

JOB 42:1-6

There is only one right response for creation to the Creator. It's actionable repentance. That's it. This means we confess our smallness before a big God, and then we start behaving like the creation and not the Creator.

While in Job's first response he acknowledges that he needs to shut his mouth and speak no further, more is required of him. In these verses, Job does just that. Job is even willing to perpetually stay in his present circumstances, ashes and all, because he realizes how foolish he has been. Now that is a man with a selfless heart. He moves from a man mourning the loss of things, to mourning the loss of himself. This is a big move. This is rock-bottom. This is realizing that we are small and God is big. Here is where a man is transformed from trying to be his own man to becoming God's man.

One word best describes this response: *repentance*.

It's not just remorse for wrongdoing. It's not just recognizing he has misspoken. It's a change in attitude and action. Notice that in this text Job's attitude is devoid of self-centeredness and the focus now moves to being entirely focused on God. Notice that in action he is now delighted to stay perpetually in his present state. This demonstrates the status of his motivation and heart.

While we dislike these moments in life this is where men are made great: bowed before the feet of the Creator himself. Thus we refuse the right to be the Creator and we focus on being the creation. By repentance, we reconcile with the God we've been in a contest with, the limitless God.

Repentance is simple when a man is brought low. Repentance involves three things. First, we verbalize a sin to God. Second, we own the effects of this sin on us and others. And third, we commit to leaving that sin behind. Charles Spurgeon said this way.

"Repentance is a discovery of the evil of sin, a mourning that we have committed it, a resolution to forsake it."

And this is where an old life ends and a new one begins. And it results in this.

LESSON FOUR | GOD'S RESPONSE TO MAN

Listen to the results in Job 42:10-11:

> *And the Lord restored the fortunes of Job, when he had prayed for his friends. And the Lord gave Job twice as much as he had before. Then came to him all his brothers and sisters and all who had known him before, and ate bread with him in his house. And they showed him sympathy and comforted him for all the evil that the Lord had brought upon him. And each of them gave him a piece of money and a ring of gold.*
>
> **JOB 42:10-11**

It's easy to read this and assume that when we repent that a blessing like this should be expected. But remember, we just learned over 42 chapters that this is not case. Job has learned that his relationship with God *is* the blessing, that the blessing is in being the creation and being led by the Creator. In being the creation we are not always guaranteed material blessings. God can give and God can take away, therefore *"blessed be his name."* Which is exactly where we began in Chapter One. It's kind of interesting that Job had to relearn this. But how many things have you had to learn and relearn in your life? In the end it's really nice that Job gets twice as much as before, but this stuff (including his righteousness) has no bearing on his motivation in his relationship with the limitless God of all things. They simply don't affect him. They don't matter. Only God matters.

This is the humbling truth of being mortal man. We are not the Creator. God is. God can give and God can take away. God will do what he chooses and we as creation must fall in line with his will. And the ultimate question for us is this:

Will you live all-in for God?

Of course, God hopes we will accept him and his will for our life because it is the way we were designed to live: one hundred percent fully devoted and all-in for Him, which is the best place to live out this life. Surrendered to God.

Today might be a day for you to do that. For the first time surrendering your entire life and will to God. Or maybe you have made this commitment in the past, but you've been holding back on trusting God with some area of your life that you been trying to do your way with little success. If your way hasn't been working, why not try it God's way? He did after all create man. And as the Creator he knows how your life would best lived. Why not let him give you the direction you need by surrendering your will to his will, and then inviting his direction and leadership in your life.

This can start with a simple prayer of surrender that I am willing to pray with you right now.

God, I surrender my life and will to you. Be the leader and Lord of my life. Guide me to knowing your will for my life. Dwell in me and give me direction by your Holy Spirit. Forgive me for living and selfish and self-centered life. Forgive me of my sin. Call me your child and may I live every day for you in all I do. Amen.

And remember: live all in for Him who lived all in for you.

REFLECTION & DISCUSSION QUESTIONS:

- Which of the four lessons stood out the most to you? Why?
- What do you need to do differently?
- How can you start the process of change today?

DEVOTIONALS FOR JOB 26-42

THE THUNDER OF GREAT POWER

But the thunder of his power who can understand?

JOB 26:14

There are things in this life that we will never fully comprehend, God is foremost among them. Job still knows (in chapter 26 nonetheless) that understanding God is out of his reach. He knows that just the sound of his power is more than his mind can understand.

On this side of heaven, it is impossible to know all that we want to know about God. While this makes us all uncomfortable, God always lets a man know just enough. Enough that we can come to a conclusion about him by faith. And yet, he discloses his power to us in amounts that both terrify and humble us about who he is and what he can do. He daily allows us to see a little more of him, which increases our faith. Faith that will carry us through any struggle this life will offer.

Job was a man who struggled more than most of us ever will. He demonstrates that God is still mightier than any challenge that may come our way. The question I believe Job poses to all men is this: do you want to see great power? If you do, then you need to trust in a great God through great struggle!

I ask you, do you really want to know the power of an Almighty God?

ASK THIS: Do you really want to know God's power?

DO THIS: Get ready.

PRAY THIS: God, dare I ask you to show me your power today?

WHEN YOU RUN OUT OF THINGS TO SAY

The words of Job are ended.

JOB 31:40

Now we might want to dismiss these six words as parenthetical, but I found this addition in the text interesting. Just like the three men (Eliphaz, Bildad, and Zophar), Job has exhausted himself. His processing, explaining, and defending are done. We end where this whole conversation began: in silence.

I don't know if you have had one of these moments in your life, but they are pretty powerful. They are moments where we are so overwhelmed that we don't know what to say. Our minds cannot process and our hearts are overwhelmed. We experience moments like these at the birth of a child or at the death of a loved one. Or like Job here, in the middle of an overwhelming crisis

Sometimes it's good to be silent. To turn off the noise. To stop the busyness. To stop inputting data. To rest our weary hearts. To shut our mouths and just be silent.

Mother Teresa once said:

In the silence of the heart God speaks. If you face God in prayer and silence, God will speak to you. Then you will know that you

are nothing. It is only when you realize your nothingness, your emptiness, that God can fill you with Himself.

ASK THIS: Where is the noise in your life?

DO THIS: Be silent.

PRAY THIS: God, speak into the void of my silence.

HOW TO SPEAK UP WHEN YOU ARE FIRED UP

> *Then Elihu the son of Barachel the Buzite, of the family of Ram, burned with anger. He burned with anger at Job because he justified himself rather than God. He burned with anger also at Job's three friends because they had found no answer, although they had declared Job to be in the wrong. Now Elihu had waited to speak to Job because they were older than he. And when Elihu saw that there was no answer in the mouth of these three men, he burned with anger.*
>
> **JOB 32:2-5**

So as we come close to the end of the story, we discover someone else present. There was a younger man: Elihu. And we see that he is brewing to speak and that he is pretty angry about a couple of things. First, that Job justified his righteousness to these men. And while Job was right that he had done nothing wrong to deserve the suffering, Elihu determines Job's response was overly focused on his righteousness instead of God's righteousness. Second, he is pretty angry that Eliphaz, Bildad, and Zophar have come up with no answer. In the end, both parties have elevated themselves a little too much. And Elihu's anger is justified, and his assessment is spot on.

Elihu is respectful in how he handles himself, even in his anger. The text says he *"waited to speak to Job because they were older than he."*

For some reason, it appears we have lost touch with this kind of respect. But this is more than just patriarchal respect for elders. This is respect combined with extraordinary restraint when an injustice has been done to the sovereignty of God. Elihu has just listened to four men bloviate about their views on God, suffering, sin, retribution, righteousness, unrighteousness, punishment, blessing, and repentance. And I am sure the whole time Elihu's been slowly boiling. As he listens, he might even hope that they would come to some godly conclusion on the matter. They drift from a conclusion to no conclusion. After they are finally silent and have run out of things to say, then Elihu speaks. And in the verses that follow, we are going to hear some great insights from a fired-up young man who is deeply passionate about a very high view of God. The best part is that we are going to learn all of them from a younger man. I think this one line, "Elihu waited to speak to Job because they were older than he," makes everything that he's about to say easier to hear.

Are you fired up about an injustice to God? There is a lot to be fired up about today. If so, be respectful, use restraint, and speak up when the time is right, and God may use you to say something rememberable.

ASK THIS: What injustice do you need to speak about?

DO THIS: Be respectful and use restraint, and then speak up for God, not yourself.

PRAY THIS: God, help me to know what to say and how to say it.

WOULD YOU SPEAK DIFFERENT IF GOD SPOKE NEXT?

*Therefore I say, 'Listen to me;
let me also declare my opinion.'*

JOB 32:10

Elihu is ready to speak and declare his opinion. For the next six chapters, this young man is going to take us on a wonderful journey through his explanation of what God is doing in Job's life and all of life. He begins by telling Job his assessment is wrong, and he needs to quiet himself and listen to a better explanation. He then dismantles his self-proclaimed righteousness and condemns Job for saying such things. He then adds that no man is righteous. Even if we were righteous, even our best righteous gift is not a gift fit for God. This ascends in proclaiming the greatness of God. And that God's righteousness, purity, holiness, wisdom, power, understanding, riches, and majesty have no end. And that they stretch beyond our ability to understand.

His words are so impressive that two events occur. First, Job sits stunned in silence. Job never speaks a word. Second, as Elihu finishes his explanation, God begins to speak. It's as if Elihu was introducing the featured keynote speaker of the day and thus hands him the mic. And God never once reprimands Elihu for anything he has said. He picks up right where Elihu left off,

GOD INTERROGATES JOB: FOUR LESSONS

which I think is a pretty strong affirmation of everything he has said to Job.

So this made me wonder. How differently would I say things if I knew that God was going to speak next? How differently would I speak to an employee, boss, or vendor? How differently would I speak to my wife, children, and mother-in-law? How differently would I speak on social media, on the freeway, or on the golf course?

Let's assume God is going to speak next, that in every conversation, God went next. And let's see if we would say any differently.

ASK THIS: Who are you going to speak differently to today?

DO THIS: As you speak to them today, imagine that God speaks next.

PRAY THIS: God, may I represent you in all I think, do, and say.

MAKE MUCH OF THE RIGHT ONE

Behold, in this you are not right. I will answer you, for God is greater than man.

JOB 33:12

This one verse sums up the core issue with all sin. When we sin, we do so because we have made more of ourselves and less of God. Elihu claims that Job has done just that somewhere in this day, made too much of himself.

But remember, before this day, scripture is clear that through all the events of his suffering, "Job did not sin or charge God with wrong." (Job 1:22) Add to this that God proclaimed that Satan acted against Job "without reason." (Job 2:3) This implies that something devious has happened during this conversation with the three friends. If you go back a read, you will see signs that Job is making a little too much of himself. It sounds like Elihu has identified it. In fact, he is going to reference specific statements of Job as his evidence and proof.

I don't know about you but I sense this at work in my life all the time. Sometimes sin is not obvious. It's just me making a little too much of myself. It's me making too much of my abilities, accomplishments, and adventures to others. Too much of my experience, efforts, and energies online. It's too much of me in what I think, say, and do. This is what is so insidious and devious about sin: its beginnings are not so obvious. It's just me making a little too much of me. And you making a little too much of you.

So today, take some time to assess this. Ask yourself, "Self, where am I too focused on me?" And then, before it gets out of hand, make a little less of yourself and a little more of God.

ASK THIS: Where in your life are you too focused on yourself?

DO THIS: Make a little less of yourself in this area.

PRAY THIS: God, be greater in my life today.

WHEN YOU GET PLAYED BACK

> *For Job has said, 'I am in the right,*
> *and God has taken away my right;*
> *in spite of my right I am counted a liar;*
> *my wound is incurable, though I am without*
> *transgression.'*
>
> **JOB 34:5-6**

When I read this today, it made me think about those arguments I sometimes have at home. You know, those ones where your wife corners you about something you've said. She plays back word-for-word a statement you've made with a little different emphasis and adds in a different perspective, and suddenly you feel trapped.

Have you ever had one of those moments? I have! I say stupid things sometimes.

This made me wonder how Job is receiving this playback about the things he's said—from a younger man nonetheless. We really don't know because Job never gets a chance to respond to Elihu. But we know this. In a few minutes, God is going to speak. God is going heap on additional emphasis and perspective. God is not going to playback anything. He is going to explain his infinite power, might, and holiness. And Job is going to be reminded of his mortality.

You see, here's my issue: when I am attacked, I become defensive. Defensiveness is an attempt to make myself bigger. Instead of trying to make myself bigger, I need to remember that God is bigger. And that I need to go smaller.

So the next time your words and mortality confront you, try going small and let God go big. He is all the defense you need. And he may not come to your defense in the timing you want, but this does not mean his sovereignty is not working. It's just not working at your speed.

ASK THIS: How can you go small today?

DO THIS: Let God be big.

PRAY THIS: God, be sovereign in my life today. Be bigger than the situations before me.

DRESS FOR ACTION LIKE A MAN

> *Then the Lord answered Job out of the whirlwind
> and said:
> "Who is this that darkens counsel by words
> without knowledge?
> Dress for action like a man;
> I will question you, and you make it known to me.*
>
> **JOB 38:1-3**

So at the end of the drama God takes center stage. Job has been through a major ordeal. But the ordeal just became more significant. A whirlwind appears out of which God's voice thunders. God ignores everyone and focuses all his attention on Job. God is about to present him with a litany of questions. Unanswerable questions.

And then his thundering voice states this, *"Dress for action like a man!"*

Every time I read this, it just sends chills down my spine. I cannot imagine hearing it from God. But eventually, we will all face this encounter. We will all hear his voice. Jesus says this about this day.

> *When the Son of Man comes in his glory, and all the angels with him, then he will sit on his glorious throne. Before him will be gathered all the nations, and he will separate people one from another as a shepherd separates the sheep from the goats.*
>
> **MATTHEW 25:31-32**

Since we know this day is coming for us all, today is the day to prepare. Now: not later. We must be dressed for action. And the prophet Isaiah tells us how to dress for this moment. He states:

> *I will greatly rejoice in the Lord;*
> *my soul shall exult in my God,*
> *for he has clothed me with the garments of salvation;*
> *he has covered me with the robe of righteousness.*
>
> **ISAIAH 61:10**

The only way to dress for action and stand before God is to clothe yourself in his righteousness and not your own.

ASK THIS: Are you ready to stand before God?

DO THIS: Cover yourself in his righteousness, not your own.

PRAY THIS: God, forgive me for trusting in my righteousness. Make your righteousness mine own.

WEIGH YOURSELF

> *Where were you when I laid the foundation of the earth?*
> *Tell me, if you have understanding.*
> *Who determined its measurements—surely you know!*
> *Or who stretched the line upon it?*
> *On what were its bases sunk,*
> *or who laid its cornerstone.*
>
> **JOB 38:4-6**

I wonder how it must have felt to be interrogated like this by the thundering voice of the Almighty God? Probably a mixture of terrifying and awesome at the same time.

Nonetheless, for the next four chapters, what God does is hurl question after question at Job. Questions for which he will have no answer. They are intended to be impossible questions. They allow Job to understand how he has overplayed himself. How he has embellished his knowledge and righteousness before his friends and thus God.

We learn from Job we have to weigh our understanding of ourselves on balance all the time. Some days we think too little of ourselves and thus underplay the power of God dwelling in us. Other days we think too much of ourselves and thus overplay that we are as great as gods. Each of us has a tipping point on the fulcrum between the two. Something that tips us toward underplaying or overplaying. This needs constant attention in our lives. We must give attention to the tip of the scale. We do this by daily weighing ourselves. Weighing our egos on the balance before God.

Every way of a man is right in his own eyes, but the Lord weighs the heart.

PROVERBS 21:2

Take a few minutes a few times today to weigh yourself. Step on the scale before the Almighty God and align yourself to his way.

ASK THIS: Have you weighed your heart today? Which way are you tipping? Underplaying? Overplaying?

DO THIS: Get back in balance before God interrogates you.

PRAY THIS: God, help me to find my way in your way. May I lean on you for understanding. Weigh me today.

THE SARCASM OF GOD

> *Where is the way to the dwelling of light,*
> *and where is the place of darkness,*
> *that you may take it to its territory*
> *and that you may discern the paths to its home?*
> *You know, for you were born then,*
> *and the number of your days is great!*
>
> **JOB 38:19-21**

Long before anything existed, there was God, and not man. This is because a Creator must exist before all things!

God existed before light and before darkness. It was God who formed, created, and spoke light into existence. God by his own choice and power created all forms of electromagnetic radiation and the visible form that we call light. Not just light itself, but how it forms and moves. It is the first thing God spoke into space and time. And still today our greatest of scientists do not fully understand it. But God understands it. Thus God enjoys the right to give Job a sarcastic response given his limited knowledge.

At no point will our age, wisdom, power, and knowledge match God's. But for some reason, as God points out to Job, we have moments when we think it does. We have these brief moments of greatness. With them come these momentary thoughts that we are great. But don't fall for the lie buried in that momentary thought. That is, unless you want to hear the sarcasm of God.

ASK THIS: Do you have any momentary thoughts of greatest?

DO THIS: Confess them before you hear the sarcasm of God.

PRAY THIS: God, I bring everything that is great and not great about me to you.

YOU WILL SOAR

> *Is it by your understanding that the hawk soars*
> *and spreads his wings toward the south?*
> *Is it at your command that the eagle mounts up*
> *and makes his nest on high?*
>
> **JOB 39:26-27**

Today we *do* understand how these great birds soar. It's by two types of updrafts. The first is called a thermal updraft, which results from the sun producing energy that heats the earth's surface, creating rising warm air. This warm air forms into unseen columns of heat around which these great birds circle, and thus soar. So the next time you see a bird circling and rising, you'll know that they are circling a thermal updraft. The second is known as an orographic updraft. These are a result of winds deflected upward by structures. Wind moves across a structure like a cliff that creates an updraft that allows a bird to soar.

While we might understand how these birds soar, it is not "by our understanding" that they soar. We cannot by sheer mental will make these things happen. We don't will the Sun into existence. Or will the Sun to produce heat. Or will a perfect amount of the Sun's energy to the surface of the Earth. Or will a column of heated air into place. But God can. And from this, God wants us to understand that our understanding is very, very, very, very, very limited. It's is limited to understanding myopic things already created and we have no power to create "by our understanding."

When we don't understand the challenges and obstacles before us, we should trust God more, not less. Rather than exerting so much effort to ploy through or trying so hard to understand, we should trust in the updrafts that God puts before us. Sometimes, while it looks like we are flying into the flame and massive cliffs, God might be providing us with time to soar "by his understanding." An understanding that is always greater than ours.

How do you need to trust God's understanding today? Consider this, and then soar by his power and will.

ASK THIS: How do you need to trust God's understanding?

DO THIS: Trust God, not your own understanding.

PRAY THIS: God, you get it. I don't. I will trust you today. May I soar on wings like eagles!

COMPARISONS THAT AFFECT OUR PERCEPTIONS

> *Then Job answered the Lord and said:*
> *"Behold, I am of small account; what shall I answer you?*
> *I lay my hand on my mouth.*
> *I have spoken once, and I will not answer;*
> *twice, but I will proceed no further."*
>
> **JOB 40:3-5**

Notice here how Job changes his posture. Previously he blustered to his friends about his innocence, righteousness, and need for a hearing from God. With every rebuttal, his speeches became longer and longer. But now, after God challenges his perception, the bluster ends. Job acknowledges he no longer needs a hearing from God. And now, when he does speak, he mumbles a reply from behind the hand that covers his mouth.

This is the danger of human comparison. We end up basing our worth or righteousness on social measurement. Thus we feel better when we do better than others. We do this because social comparison positively affects our esteem. Slowly we establish our identity in these social comparisons. As a result we perceive too much of ourselves. Self-esteem is not God's way to be esteemed; it's only the path to narcissism. So God reminds us through the interrogation of Job that we need always give attention to the comparisons that affect our perceptions.

We are reminded the only place to perceive our identity is in God.

Today consider what area in your life where you have made a comparison. Cast that thought aside and get your perceptions right. Be esteemed by God and not your own efforts.

ASK THIS: With whom or where have you made too many comparisons?

DO THIS: Get your perceptions in order.

PRAY THIS: God, reveal my comparison and get my perceptions in order.

REPENTANCE — WHERE MEN ARE MADE GREAT

Then Job answered the Lord and said:
"I know that you can do all things,
and that no purpose of yours can be thwarted.
'Who is this that hides counsel without knowledge?'
Therefore I have uttered what I did not understand,
things too wonderful for me, which I did not know.
'Hear, and I will speak;
I will question you, and you make it known to me.'
I had heard of you by the hearing of the ear,
but now my eye sees you;
therefore I despise myself,
and repent in dust and ashes."

JOB 42:1-6

This final acknowledgment by Job is profound. There are two things that Job acknowledges after God finishes his interrogation. First, Job acknowledges the limits of his understanding. Second, Job acknowledges his self-righteousness and increased boldness. What results from both acknowledgments is a man who now goes low. His attitude and position have changed. His arrogance and self-righteousness are gone. He is now satisfied to sit perpetually in the dust and ashes mourning all he has lost. He acknowledges that he is a mere creature and is no contest for the Creator.

While we dislike these moments in life, this is where men are made great, right before the throne of the Almighty God. Exposure and brokenness result in contentment and meaning. It's through repentance that we reconcile with the only person we have actually been in a contest with: none other than Almighty God.

Take some time today to repent. Even five minutes right now. Repent by doing this:

- *First, verbalize a sin to God.*
- *Second, own the effects of this sin.*
- *Third, commit to leaving it behind.*

Charles Spurgeon once said this:

"Repentance is a discovery of the evil of sin, a mourning that we have committed it, a resolution to forsake it."

ASK THIS: What sin do you need to verbalize to God?

DO THIS: Take five minutes to walk through the three steps above.

PRAY THIS: God, may I be humble and repentant before you this day.

RUNNING TO REPENTANCE TOGETHER

> *After the Lord had spoken these words to Job, the Lord said to Eliphaz the Temanite: "My anger burns against you and against your two friends, for you have not spoken of me what is right, as my servant Job has. Now therefore take seven bulls and seven rams and go to my servant Job and offer up a burnt offering for yourselves. And my servant Job shall pray for you, for I will accept his prayer not to deal with you according to your folly. For you have not spoken of me what is right, as my servant Job has." So Eliphaz the Temanite and Bildad the Shuhite and Zophar the Naamathite went and did what the Lord had told them, and the Lord accepted Job's prayer.*
>
> **JOB 42:7-9**

Here we learn that Job is not the only one in need of repentance. Eliphaz, Bildad, and Zophar have some business to address as well. And it's interesting how God wants them to reconcile it. He invites them to ask the brother they have offended to bring the burnt offering and sacrifice for them. This is ironic since this is what they determined that Job needed to do. But with this, two things happen. First, they are reconciled to God. Second, they are reconciled to each other. I think we are all tempted to run from Christian community during hard times. God shows us that this is exactly the wrong thing to do. Both parties should graciously step toward the tension. Catch this: when God-fearing men come together in penance and prayer, God's glory is accomplished. God takes our imperfections and they become a perfect witness for Him. Still, today, as we read the book of Job, we see God's glory displayed as a testimony through four types of imperfect men.

Today consider this question. Who is that person you are running from that you need to run to? Seek them out, and pursue the grace of God together.

ASK THIS: Who is that person you are running from that you need to run to?

DO THIS: Pursue God's grace together.

PRAY THIS: God, I need your grace. But I also need the strength to pursue a relationship with a follower in the faith. I recognize you want me to pursue them today. May they be receptive. And together, may you receive our need for forgiveness and mercy.

THE FOCUS OF CONTENTMENT

> And the Lord restored the fortunes of Job, when he had prayed for his friends. And the Lord gave Job twice as much as he had before. Then came to him all his brothers and sisters and all who had known him before, and ate bread with him in his house. And they showed him sympathy and comforted him for all the evil that the Lord had brought upon him. And each of them gave him a piece of money and a ring of gold.
>
> And the Lord blessed the latter days of Job more than his beginning. And he had 14,000 sheep, 6,000 camels, 1,000 yoke of oxen, and 1,000 female donkeys. He had also seven sons and three daughters. And he called the name of the first daughter Jemimah, and the name of the second Keziah, and the name of the third Keren-happuch. And in all the land there were no women so beautiful as Job's daughters. And their father gave them an inheritance among their brothers. And after this Job lived 140 years, and saw his sons, and his sons' sons, four generations. And Job died, an old man, and full of days.
>
> **JOB 42:10-17**

This is such a spectacular ending to a story of spectacular suffering. I really don't have much to add to what the author has written, except maybe this one thing. We have to remember that it's easy to get hypnotized by all the stuff we read about at the end of the story. But the story's point is that life is not about the stuff, whether we have it or not. It's only about one thing—God. It's about God, regardless of whether we live in want or plenty.

The apostle Paul said it this way:

> *Not that I am speaking of being in need, for I have learned in whatever situation I am to be content. I know how to be brought low, and I know how to abound. In any and every circumstance, I have learned the secret of facing plenty and hunger, abundance and need. I can do all things through him who strengthens me.*
>
> **PHILIPPIANS 4:11-13**

If you feel discontentment today (which you may) you may want to determine if this discontentment comes from being content with the wrong things. If it does, then turn from trusting in these things and trust in God and his strength. Because God's strength is strong enough to do all things. It was for Job. It did for Paul. And it will do the same for you.

ASK THIS: In what are you trying to find your contentment?

DO THIS: Be content in God. He is strong.

PRAY THIS: God, satisfy my discontent heart!